The
SEARCH FOR
SIGNIFICANCE
Devotional

The SEARCH FOR SIGNIFICANCE *DEVOTIONAL*

DAILY MEDITATIONS, REFLECTIONS, & PRAYERS

ROBERT S. MCGEE

Rapha
PUBLISHING

Houston, Texas

WORD PUBLISHING
Dallas·London·Vancouver·Melbourne

THE SEARCH FOR SIGNIFICANCE DEVOTIONAL: *DAILY MEDITATIONS, REFLECTIONS, & PRAYERS*
by Robert S. McGee

Unless otherwise indicated, Scripture quotations are from the NEW AMERICAN STANDARD BIBLE, © The Lockman Foundation 1960, 1962, 1963, 1968, 1971, 1972, 1973, 1975, 1977.

Scripture quotations noted NIV are taken from the HOLY BIBLE: NEW INTERNATIONAL VERSION. © 1973, 1978, 1984, International Bible Society.

Portions of *The Search for Significance* book and workbook have been reprinted and adapted with permission of the author.

Second Printing, 1993
ISBN: 0-945276-41-9
Printed in the United States of America

ACKNOWLEDGMENT_____

I WANT TO THANK SANDY BALLARD FOR HER EXCELLENT WORK and outstanding contribution to this devotional. Sandy provided editorial assistance, compiled the prayers at the end of each day, and attractively designed the layout for this book. Her efforts have added to both the contents and the appearance of this work.

INTRODUCTION _____

SEVERAL YEARS AGO, A STUDY WAS CONDUCTED BY A MAJOR seminary to determine which factors encourage spiritual growth. Many spiritual disciplines were examined, such as church attendance, regular Bible study, and prayer. One factor, however, proved to have the greatest influence in encouraging people to grow in their relationships with God: meditation. Consistent reflection on God's Word had a far greater impact than any other discipline.

This devotional is designed to stimulate and enhance that kind of consistent reflection. Each week consists of five daily studies, including a weekend journal to help you assimilate the concepts, truths, and ideas from the previous week. Also, each day contains a reflection question or two and a "prayer starter" to help you express your desires, feelings, and needs to the Lord.

Some of us feel undue stress when we look at a daily devotional because we think if we don't "keep up," we are not being spiritual enough—that we are somehow failing in our walk with the Lord. Consistency is laudable and good, but don't worry of you miss a day or if your weekend journal ends in the middle of a week. The goal is to reflect on God's truth so that it sinks deeply into our hearts and minds. The pace is not as important as the depth of our reflection.

Above all, this devotional is a book of hope. I trust that God will use it to encourage you to grasp His love and grace more deeply than ever before. And too, I trust that His love will then have a profound impact on every aspect of your life!

ROBERT S. McGEE

DAY 1 _____

TRUE FREEDOM

You shall know the truth, and the truth shall make you free.

JOHN 8:32

IN THIS PASSAGE, CHRIST WAS REFERRING NOT ONLY TO AN intellectual assent to the truth, but also to the application of truth in the most basic issues of life: our goals, our motives, and our sense of self-worth. Unfortunately, many of us give only lip-service to the powerful truths of the Scriptures without allowing them to affect the basis of our self-esteem in a radical way. Instead, we continue to seek our security and purpose from worldly sources: personal success, status, beauty, wealth, and the approval of others. These rewards may fulfill us for a short time, but they soon lead us to a sense of urgency to succeed and be approved again.

To meet these compelling needs, we drive ourselves to achieve, doing virtually anything to make people happy with us, and spend countless hours and dollars trying to look "just right." Often, we avoid situations and people where the risks of failure and rejection are high. It's a rat race that can't be won by simply running faster. We need to get off of this hopeless treadmill, and learn to apply the foundational truths that can motivate us to live for Christ rather than for the approval of other people.

1

Christ's death paid the penalty for our sins, and His resurrection gives us new life, new goals, and new hope. He has given us complete security and challenging purpose. These are not based on our abilities, but on His grace and the power of His Spirit. Yes, Christ wants us to be zealous and ambitious, but not about our success or status. If we understand His forgiveness and acceptance, we will pursue the right things—Christ and His cause—and we will be free to enjoy His love.

• What difference would it make in your attitude, relationships, and goals if you grasped the reality that your worth is not conditional (i.e., based on performance), but is based on the truth of the unconditional love, forgiveness, and acceptance of God?

Thank You for loving me, Father. As I become more aware of how complete I am in You, please help me to . . .

DAY 2 _____

TURNING ON THE LIGHT

The Lord is my light and my salvation;
    Whom shall I fear?
The Lord is the defense of my life;
    Whom shall I dread?
              PSALM 27:1

WE ALL HAVE EXPERIENCED THE INABILITY TO BE OBJECTIVE about our experiences, thoughts, and behavior in different circumstances. This objective "light" didn't begin to penetrate my own life until shortly after I had entered the business world. Before that time, whenever I felt the pain of rejection, the sting of sarcasm, or anything less than the complete approval of others, I tried to shrug it off. I reasoned that because of my status as a Christian, I should exude an attitude of happiness and contentment in all things. When something didn't go the way I'd hoped or planned it would, I simply told myself it didn't really matter. Though I was able to fool myself in these instances, my gloomy countenance told those who were closest to me another story.

On one such occasion, a good friend of mine inquired about what was wrong. "You seem troubled," he said. "Is anything bothering you?"

"Me? No, I'm fine."

"You don't seem fine to me," he persisted. "You're acting as though you might be depressed about something."

3

I stuck to my time-tested text. "No, really, I *am* fine. I guess I've just been a little pressured lately."

The truth was that an idea I'd presented in a business meeting the week before had been challenged and later, shot down. I didn't think it really mattered at first, but after hearing my friend's remarks, I began to wonder if I were being honest with myself.

Several weeks later, I phoned this friend to thank him for confronting me about my behavior. I briefly told him about the business meeting and said, "Realizing I was hurt because my idea was rejected has enabled me to be honest with the Lord about my feelings and begin working through them."

"I'm sorry about what happened," he said, "but I appreciate your honesty, and think it's great that you're doing something constructive with a difficult situation."

Over time, I began to confide in this friend about other problems I encountered. He helped me a great deal. At times, he would say, "Here's how I'd feel in your situation. I'd be angry because . . . . Do *you* feel angry?" Or, "I'd be hurt because . . . . Do *you* feel hurt?"

In the light of his honesty and love, and through the gracious work of the Holy Spirit, I began to be honest with myself and with God. The tough exterior I had developed started cracking, and I began to experience the pain I had neither wanted nor allowed myself to feel. This was hardly pleasant, but acknowledging the presence of hurt in my life was my first step toward finding comfort.

———

• What are some reasons people are afraid of the truth about themselves?

Sometimes being honest with You, myself, and others can be painful. Thank You, Jesus, for Your never-ending comfort. Today, I'm feeling . . .

DAY 3 _____

STAYING IN THE DARK

Teach me what I cannot see;
if I have done wrong, I will not do so again.
JOB 34:32, NIV

WHY DO SOME OF US LACK OBJECTIVITY? WHY CAN'T WE SEE the reality of our lives? Why are we afraid to "turn on the lights"?

There are a number of answers to these questions, and they vary for each person. Perhaps we think that our situations are "normal," that experiencing loneliness, hurt, and anger is really all there is to life. Perhaps we want to be "good Christians," and believing that *good* Christians don't have problems or feelings like ours, we deny the existence of our painful emotions. Perhaps our lack of objectivity is a learned response from childhood. All of us desperately want our parents to be loving and supportive. If ours aren't (or weren't), we may protect our concept of them by blaming ourselves for their lack of love, and deny that we have been hurt by their behavior.

• In what ways is "darkness" more comfortable than "light"?

- What are some ways you can tell if you are being objective or not?

- How would increased objectivity affect your life and relationships?

Father, thank You for the lessons You're teaching me about my emotions. As I strive to be more objective, I need You to . . .

DAY 4 _____

CONFRONTING REALITY

Search me, O God, and know my heart;
  Try me and know my anxious thoughts;
And see if there be any hurtful way in me,
  And lead me in the everlasting way.
                    PSALM 139:23–24

HUMAN BEINGS DEVELOP ELABORATE DEFENSE MECHANISMS TO block pain and gain significance. We suppress emotions; we are compulsive perfectionists; we drive ourselves to succeed, or withdraw and become passive; we attack people who hurt us; we punish ourselves when we fail; we try to say clever things to be accepted; we help people so that we will be appreciated; and we say and do countless other things.

A sense of need usually propels us to look for an alternative. We may have the courage to examine ourselves and may desperately want to change, but may be unsure of how and where to start. We may refuse to look honestly within for fear of what we'll find, or we may be afraid that even if we can discover what's wrong, nothing can help us.

It is difficult—if not impossible—to turn on the light of objectivity by ourselves. We need guidance from the Holy Spirit, as well as the honesty, love, and encouragement of at least one other person who's willing to help us. Even then, we may become depressed as we begin to discover the effects of our wounds. Some of us have deep emotional and spiritual scars resulting from the neglect, abuse, and manipulation that often accompany living in a dysfunctional family (alcoholism, drug abuse, divorce, absent father or mother, excessive anger, verbal and/or physical abuse, etc.), but all of us bear the effects of our own sinful nature and the imperfections of others.

Whether your hurts are deep or relatively mild, it is wise to be honest about them in the context of affirming relationships so that healing can begin.

――――――――

- Describe your need for healing. What is your family background? How did (does) your relationship with your parents affect you? Have you experienced deep wounds, mild abrasions, or something in-between?

Please help me to have the courage to look at myself objectively—to be honest about my need to change and heal. As I try to be more like You, Jesus, please show me . . .

9

DAY 5 _____

AT THE DEEPEST LEVEL

Surely you desire truth in the inner parts;
you teach me wisdom in the inmost place.
PSALM 51:6, NIV

MANY OF US MISTAKENLY BELIEVE THAT GOD DOESN'T WANT US to be honest about our lives. We think that He will be upset with us if we tell Him how we really feel. But the Scriptures tell us that God does not want us to be superficial—in our relationship with Him, with others, or in our own lives.

The Lord desires truth and honesty at the deepest level, and wants us to experience His love, forgiveness, and power in *all* areas of our lives. Experiencing His love does not mean that all of our thoughts, emotions, and behaviors will be pleasant and pure. It means that we can be *real*, feeling pain and joy, love and anger, confidence and confusion.

The Psalms give us tremendous insight about what it means to be honest with the Lord. David and other psalmists wrote and spoke honestly about the full range of their responses to situations.

10

- Read Psalm 51:6. Why do you think that the Lord wants us to be honest?

I realize that even before I think or speak, You already know what is in my heart. You know if my thoughts, words, and actions are honest portrayals of my feelings. I'm grateful for Your omniscience, Lord. Realizing that You already know the truth helps me to not be afraid of reaching toward deeper levels of honesty with myself. I am comforted in knowing that You are already at the next level, waiting for me to arrive. In my awareness of this, I confess . . .

11

JOURNAL _____ WEEK 1

From my reflection this week, I learned . . .

   . . . about God.

   . . . about myself.

   . . . about my motivations.

One thing I want to apply is:

Lord, I hope . . .

Lord, I need you to . . .

DAY 6 _____

PRESUMPTIONS

Through presumption comes nothing but strife,
But with those who receive counsel is wisdom.
PROVERBS 13:10

SOME PEOPLE BEGIN MOVING TOWARD HEALING AND HEALTH
rather quickly. Others, however, may read and study, go
to seminars and meetings—they may even be in
relationships where they are loved and encouraged—but
they may not see substantive change in their lives and
patterns of behavior. One reason for this spiritual and
emotional inertia is a sense of hopelessness. For various
reasons (family background, past experiences, poor role-
modeling), we may have negative presumptions which
determine our receptivity to love and truth. In some
cases, God's light may have revealed our pain and wall of
defenses, but it may not yet have penetrated to our deepest
thoughts and beliefs about ourselves. These beliefs may
not be clearly articulated, but often reflect misperceptions
such as these:

- God doesn't really care about me.
- I am an unlovable, worthless person. Nobody will
  ever love me.
- I'll never be able to change.
- I've been a failure all my life. I guess I'll always be
  a failure.

- If people really knew me, they wouldn't like me.

When the light of love and honesty shines on thoughts of hopelessness, it is often very painful. We begin to admit that we really do feel negatively about ourselves— and have for a long time. But God's love, expressed through His people, and woven into our lives by His Spirit and His Word can, over a period of time, bring healing even to our deepest wounds and instill within us an appropriate sense of self-worth.

- Read 2 Timothy 3:16–17 and explain how the Scriptures can affect our thinking and our lives.

When I'm feeling hopeless, God, please give me a gentle reminder of Your presence. Thinking of You— knowing that You created me—helps me to remember that I am a very special person. This makes me feel . . .

DAY 7 _____

SEARCHING FOR SIGNIFICANCE

Now on the last day, the great day of the feast, Jesus stood and cried out, saying, "If any man is thirsty, let him come to Me and drink. He who believes in Me, as the Scripture said, 'From his innermost being shall flow rivers of living water.'" But this He spoke of the Spirit, whom those who believed in Him were to receive; for the Spirit was not yet given, because Jesus was not yet glorified.

JOHN 7:37–39

RELATIVELY FEW OF US EXPERIENCE THE BLEND OF CONTENTMENT and godly intensity that God desires for each person. From life's outset, we find ourselves on the prowl, searching to satisfy some inner, unexplained yearning. Our hunger causes us to search for people who will love us. Our desire for acceptance pressures us to perform for the praise of others. We strive for success, driving our minds and bodies harder and farther, hoping that because of our sweat and sacrifice, others will appreciate us more.

But the man or woman who lives only for the love and attention of others is never satisfied—at least, not for long. Despite our efforts, we will never find lasting, fulfilling peace if we have to continually prove ourselves to others. Our desire to be loved and accepted is a symptom of a deeper need—the need that often governs our behavior and is the primary source of our emotional pain. Often unrecognized, this is our need for self-worth.

- *If any man is thirsty* is a metaphor for our desire and need for Christ. What does it mean to *drink* of Christ?

- In what ways are you *thirsty* for Him?

Thank You, God, for the peace that comes from knowing I no longer need to prove myself to others. As I rest in the knowledge that You accept me totally and unconditionally, I want to praise You for . . .

DAY 8 _____

THE *REAL* ABUNDANT LIFE

Put on the full armor of God, that you may be able to
stand firm against the schemes of the devil. For our
struggle is not against flesh and blood, but against the
rulers, against the powers, against the world forces of this
darkness, against the spiritual forces of wickedness in the
heavenly places.

EPHESIANS 6:11–12

IN THE SCRIPTURES, GOD SUPPLIES THE ESSENTIALS FOR DIS-
covering our true significance and worth. The first two
chapters of Genesis recount man's creation, revealing
man's intended purpose (to honor God) and man's value
(that he is a special creation of God). John 10:10 also
reminds us of how much God treasures His creation, in
that Christ came so that man might experience "abundant
life." However, as Christians, we need to realize that this
abundant life is lived in a real world filled with pain,
rejection, and failure. Therefore, experiencing the
abundant life God intends for us does not mean that our
lives will be problem-free. On the contrary, life itself is a
series of problems that often act as obstacles to our search
for significance, and the abundant life is the experience of
God's love, forgiveness, and power in the midst of these
problems. The Scriptures warn us that we live within a
warfare that can destroy our faith, lower our self-esteem,

and lead us into depression. In his letter to the Ephesians, Paul instructs us to put on the armor of God so that we can be equipped for spiritual battle. However, it often seems that unsuspecting believers are the last to know this battle is occurring, and that Christ has ultimately won the war. They are surprised and confused by difficulties, thinking that the Christian life is a playground, not a battlefield.

- How can believing that "the abundant life is freedom from problems" be a hindrance to faith?

- How is spiritual warfare a part of the abundant life?

*Father, as I grow in You, I am increasingly aware that the problems I face are accompanied by valuable lessons You want me to learn. I don't look forward to pain or misfortune, but knowing that You're there beside me, wanting to teach me something through my struggles— and that I **really** matter to You—helps me to not be afraid. Father, today I need You to . . .*

DAY 9 _____

SPECIFIC SOLUTIONS

See to it that no one takes you captive through
philosophy and empty deception, according to the tradition
of men, according to the elementary principles of the world,
rather than according to Christ.
For in Him all the fulness of Deity dwells in bodily form.
COLOSSIANS 2:8–9

As CHRISTIANS, OUR FULFILLMENT IN THIS LIFE DEPENDS NOT
on our skills to avoid life's problems, but on our ability to
apply God's specific solutions to those problems. An
accurate understanding of God's truth is the first step
toward discovering our significance and worth.
Unfortunately, many of us have been exposed to
inadequate teaching from both religious and secular
sources concerning our self-worth. As a result, we may
have a distorted self-perception, and may be experiencing
hopelessness rather than the rich and meaningful life
God intends for us.

Whether labeled "self-esteem" or "self-worth," the
feeling of significance is crucial to man's emotional,
spiritual, and social stability, and is the driving element
within the human spirit. Understanding this single need
opens the door to understanding our actions and attitudes.

What a waste to attempt to change behavior without
truly understanding the driving needs that cause such

behavior! Yet, millions of people spend a lifetime searching for love, acceptance, and success without understanding the need that compels them. We must understand that this hunger for self-worth is God-given and can only be satisfied by Him. Our value is not dependent on our ability to earn the fickle acceptance of people, but rather, its true source is the love and acceptance of God. He created us. He alone knows how to fulfill *all* of our needs.

———————

• Are you glad you are you?

• Do you have a healthy sense of self-worth?

Jesus, please show me the areas of my life where I fail to rely on You for my self-worth and, instead, look to others for acceptance. I admit . . .

21

DAY 10 _____

A REASONABLE RESPONSE

For by grace (unmerited favor) you have been saved
(rescued from spiritual death—hell) through faith (trust);
and that not of yourselves, it is the gift of God; not as a
result of works, that no one should boast.

EPHESIANS 2:8–9

ARE YOU TRUSTING IN YOUR OWN ABILITIES TO EARN ACCEPTANCE
with God, or are you trusting in the death of Christ to pay
for your sins, and the resurrection of Christ to give you
new life? Take a moment to reflect on this question: On a
scale of 0–100 percent, how sure are you that you would
spend eternity with God if you died today? An answer of
less than 100 percent may indicate that you are trusting,
at least in part, in yourself. You may be thinking, *Isn't it
arrogant to say that I am 100 percent sure?* Indeed, it would
be arrogance if you were trusting in yourself—your
abilities, your actions, and good deeds—to earn your
salvation. However, if you are no longer trusting in your
own efforts, but in the all-sufficient payment of Christ,
then 100 percent certainty is a response of humility and
thankfulness, not arrogance.

If there is any question about whether you have
conclusively accepted Christ's substitutionary death to
pay for the wrath you deserve for your sins, take some
time to think about the question we have examined, and

reflect on His love and forgiveness. Then, respond by trusting in Christ and accepting His payment for your sins. You can use this prayer to express your faith:

> Lord Jesus, I need You. I want You to be my Savior and Lord. I accept Your death on the cross as the complete payment for my sins. Thank You for forgiving me and for giving me new life. Help me to grow in my understanding of Your love and power so that my life will bring honor to You. Amen.

- On a scale of 0–100 percent, how sure are you that you would go to heaven if you died tonight?

0%__ 10%__ 25%__ 35%__ 50%__ 75%__ 85%__ 95%__ 100%__

- If you died tonight and stood before God and He asked you "Why should I let you into heaven?" what would you say?

I am overwhelmed with love for You, Lord. Your gift of salvation fills my heart with gratitude like nothing else ever could. Thank You for . . .

JOURNAL _____ WEEK 2

From my reflection this week, I learned . . .

   . . . about God.

   . . . about myself.

   . . . about my motivations.

One thing I want to apply is:

Lord, I hope . . .

Lord, I need you to . . .

DAY 11 _____

THE IMPACT OF FAITH

As [a man] thinks within himself, so he is.
PROVERBS 23:7

BECAUSE OUR PERFORMANCE AND ABILITY TO PLEASE OTHERS SO dominates our search for significance, we have difficulty recognizing the distinction between our real identity and the way we behave, a realization crucial to understanding our true worth. Our true value is not based on our behavior or the approval of others, but on what God's Word says is true of us.

Our behavior is often a reflection of our beliefs about who we are. It is usually consistent with what we think to be true about ourselves. If we base our worth solidly on the truths of God's Word, then our behavior will often reflect His love, grace, and power. But if we base our worth on our abilities or the fickle approval of others, then our behavior will reflect the insecurity, fear, and anger that comes from such instability.

Though we usually behave in ways that are consistent with our beliefs, at times, our actions may contradict them. For example, we may believe that we are generous and gracious, when we are actually very selfish. Sometimes, our behavior changes what we believe about ourselves. If, for instance, we succeed in a task at which we initially believed we would fail, our confidence may begin to grow and expand to other areas of our lives. Our feelings, behavior, and beliefs all interact to shape our lives.

Our lifestyle is usually a reflection of what we think about ourselves. Analyze your lifestyle. Describe . . .

• The things you talk about:

• The places you like to go:

• The people you spend time with:

• Your ambitions and dreams:

• How you spend your time:

• How you spend your money:

Heavenly Father, as I search myself—my motives, priorities—to discover where I have based my self-worth, I admit . . .

DAY 12 _____

DEVELOPING BELIEFS AT HOME

For evils beyond number have surrounded me;
   My iniquities have overtaken me, so that I am not able
      to see;
They are more numerous than the hairs of my head;
   And my heart has failed me.
Be pleased, O Lord, to deliver me;
   Make haste, O Lord to help me.
Let those be ashamed and humiliated together
   Who seek my life to destroy it;
Let those be turned back and dishonored
   Who delight in my hurt.

PSALM 40:12–14

OUR HOME ENVIRONMENT PLAYS A CENTRAL ROLE IN FORMING our beliefs and emotions, and these can have a powerful impact on our outlook and behavior.

This truth is evident in the case of Scott. Scott grew up in a home without praise, discouraged by his parents whenever he attempted anything new and challenging. After twenty years of hearing, "You'll never be able to do anything, Scott, so don't even try," he believed it himself. Neither Scott nor his parents could later understand why he had flunked out of college and was continually shuffling from one job to another, never able to achieve success. Believing he was doing the best he could do, but suspecting he would always fail, Scott consistently performed according to his self-perception.

Separated from God and His Word, people have only their abilities and the opinions of others on which to base their worth, and the circumstances around them ultimately control the way they feel about themselves.

• List some activities, relationships, or achievements which make you feel better about yourself:

• List some activities, poor relationships, or failures which make you feel badly about yourself:

Lord, as I reflect on the home environment in which I was raised, I feel . . .

29

DAY 13 _____

COMPULSIONS
AND WITHDRAWAL

. . . Every one who thirsts,
   come to the waters;
And you who have no money
   come, buy and eat.
Come, buy wine and milk
   Without money and without cost.
Why do you spend money for what is not bread,
   And your wages for what does not satisfy?
Listen carefully to Me, and eat what is good,
   And delight yourself in abundance.
Incline your ear and come to Me.
   Listen, that you may live;
And I will make an everlasting covenant with you,
   According to the faithful mercies shown to David.

                ISAIAH 55:1–3

WE ALL HAVE COMPELLING, GOD-GIVEN NEEDS FOR LOVE, acceptance, and purpose, and most of us will go to virtually any lengths to meet those needs. Many of us have become masters at "playing the game" to be successful and win the approval of others. Some of us, however, have failed and have experienced the pain of disapproval so often that we have given up and have withdrawn into a shell of hurt, numbness, or depression. In both cases, we are living by the deception that our worth is based on our performance and others' opinions—some of us are simply more adept at playing this game than others.

Our attempts to meet our needs for success and approval fall into two broad categories: compulsiveness and withdrawal.

Some people expend extra effort, work extra hours, and try to say just the right thing to achieve success and please those around them. These people may have a compelling desire to be in control of every situation. They are perfectionists. If a job isn't done perfectly, if they aren't dressed just right, if they aren't considered "the best" by their peers, then they work harder until they achieve that coveted status. And woe to the poor soul who gets in their way! Whoever doesn't contribute to their success and acclaim is a threat to their self-esteem—an unacceptable threat. They may be very personable and have a lot of "friends," but the goal of these relationships may not be to give encouragement and love; it may be to manipulate others to contribute to their success. That may sound harsh, but people who are driven to succeed will often use practically everything and everybody to meet that need.

The sad truth is that most perfectionists never are satisfied with their work, no matter how well their efforts have turned out. This perception of imperfection only fuels their compulsion to "do it right next time."

The other broad category is withdrawal. Those who manifest this behavior usually try to avoid failure and disapproval by avoiding risks. They won't volunteer for the jobs that offer much risk of failure. They gravitate toward people who are comforting and kind, skirting relationships that might demand vulnerability, and consequently, the risk of rejection. They may appear to be easygoing, but inside they are usually running from every potential situation or relationship that might not succeed.

Obviously, these are two broad categories. Most of us exhibit some combination of the two behaviors, willing to take risks and work hard in the areas where we feel sure of success, but avoiding the people and situations that may bring rejection and failure.

———————

• Whose opinion of you do you value most?

• What is your most common response to that person?

Father, as I search my own behavior and try to become purer in my motives, please help me to be more aware of how I may be compelling others to withdraw or "perform" as well. I admit . . .

DAY 14 _____

PARENTS AS MODELS

The Lord sustains all who fall,
And raises up all who are bowed down.
The eyes of all look to Thee,
And Thou dost give them their food in due time.
Thou dost open Thy hand,
And dost satisfy the desire of every living thing.

PSALM 145:14–16

WHEN WE BASE OUR SECURITY ON SUCCESS AND OTHERS' opinions, we become dependent on our abilities to perform and please others. We develop a *have-to* mentality: *I have to do well on this exam (or my security as a "good student" will be threatened); I have to make that deal (or it will mean that my boss will think I am a failure); My father (or mother, spouse, or friend) has to appreciate me and be happy with my decisions (because I cannot cope with his disapproval).*

Our self-esteem and view of God are usually a mirror of our parents' attitudes toward us. Those who are loved and affirmed by their parents tend to have a fairly healthy self-concept, and usually find it easy to believe that God is loving and powerful. Those whose parents have been neglectful, manipulative, or condemning usually seem to feel that they have to earn a sense of worth, and that God is aloof, demanding, and/or cruel.

Our parents are our models of the character of God. When we do not have that fundamental sense of feeling loved and protected by them, then we tend to base our self-worth on how well we perform and please others, instead of on what the sovereign God of the universe, our all-wise, omniscient Savior says of us.

• Is it difficult to view yourself in terms other than your performance or others' opinions of you? If so, why?

Father, please help me see myself through Your eyes, and show me . . .

DAY 15 _____

THE SOURCE OF OUR SECURITY

For you have not received a spirit of slavery leading to
fear again, but you have received a spirit of adoption as
sons by which we cry out, "Abba! Father!"
ROMANS 8:15

W E DO NOT *HAVE TO* BE SUCCESSFUL OR *HAVE TO* BE PLEASING
to others to have a healthy sense of self-esteem and
worth. That worth has freely and conclusively been given
to us by God. Failure and/or the disapproval of others
can't take it away! Therefore, we can conclude, *It would
be nice to be approved by my parents* (or whomever), *but if
they don't approve of me, I'm still loved and accepted by
God.* Do you see the difference? The *have-to* mentality is
sheer slavery to performance and the opinions of others,
but we are secure and free in Christ. We don't *have to*
have success or anyone else's approval. Of course, it would
be nice to have success and approval, but the point is
clear: Christ is the source of our security; Christ is the
basis of our worth; Christ is the only One who promises
and never fails.

The transition from the slavery and compulsion of a
have-to mentality to the freedom and strength of a *want-
to* motivation is a process. Bondage to such thinking is
often deeply rooted in our personalities, patterns of
behavior, and ways of relating to other people. These

patterns of thinking, feeling, and responding—learned over time—flow as naturally as the course of rainwater in a dry desert riverbed. Changing them requires time, the encouragement of others, the truth and application of God's Word, and the power of God's Spirit.

———————

• Describe how your thoughts and beliefs have been developed. (Include the influences of society, your daily background, experiences, relationships):

*Father, You are my source of security. Thank You for **always** being here with me. Thank You for . . .*

JOURNAL _____ WEEK 3

From my reflection this week, I learned . . .

   . . . about God.

   . . . about myself.

   . . . about my motivations.

One thing I want to apply is:

Lord, I hope . . .

Lord, I need you to . . .

DAY 16 _____

THE HOLY SPIRIT

"And I will ask the Father, and He will give you another
Helper, that He may be with you forever. That is the Spirit
of truth, whom the world cannot receive, because it does
not behold Him or know Him, but you know Him because
He abides with you, and will be in you."
JOHN 14:16–17

DEEP, SPIRITUAL HEALING REQUIRES GIVING ATTENTION TO THE
whole man, to his emotional, relational, physical, and
spiritual needs. The Holy Spirit is given by God to
communicate His love, light, forgiveness, and power to
our deepest needs. This spiritual aspect of healing is
perhaps the most fundamental, because our view of God
(and subsequent relationship with Him) can determine
the quality and degree of health we experience in every
other area of our lives.

Some of us believe that the Holy Spirit's ministry is
characterized only by positive, pleasant emotions like
love and joy. However, one of the miracles of the Holy
Spirit's work is that of producing honesty and courage in
our lives as we grapple with the reality of pain. He is the
Spirit of truth, not denial, and He enables us to experience
each element of the healing process as He gives us wisdom,
strength, and encouragement through God's Word and
other people.

_____

• Describe the Holy Spirit's role in the healing process:

Dear Father, I am grateful for Your . . .

DAY 17 _____

THE TRAP OF PERFORMANCE

If you have died with Christ to the elementary principles of the world, why, as if you were living in the world, do you submit yourself to decrees, such as, do not handle, do not taste, do not touch (which all refer to things destined to perish with the using)—in accordance with the commandments and teachings of men? These are matters which have, to be sure, the appearance of wisdom in self-made religion and self-abasement and severe treatment of the body, but are of no value against fleshly indulgence.

COLOSSIANS 2:20–23

BECAUSE OF OUR UNIQUE PERSONALITIES, WE EACH REACT VERY differently to this deception: *I must meet certain standards in order to feel good about myself.* As we saw in a previous chapter, some of us respond by becoming slaves to perfectionism—driving ourselves incessantly toward attaining goals.

Perfectionists can be quite vulnerable to serious mood disorders, and often anticipate rejection when they believe they haven't met the standards they are trying so hard to attain. Therefore, perfectionists tend to react defensively to criticism and demand to be in control of most situations they encounter. Because they are usually more competent than most, perfectionists see nothing wrong with their compulsions. "I just like to see things done well," they claim. There is certainly nothing inherently wrong with doing things well; the problem is that perfectionists usually base their self-worth on their ability to accomplish a goal. Therefore, failure is a threat and is totally unacceptable to them. Many high achievers are driven beyond healthy limitations. Rarely able to relax and enjoy life, they let their families and relationships suffer as they strive to accomplish often unrealistic goals.

• Why do people use performance as a measurement of personal worth?

Heavenly Father, I need to slow down today and focus on improving my present relationships. In the whirlwind activities of daily life, I confess that I get caught up with . . .

Day 18_____

THE PIT OF DESPAIR

For we also once were foolish ourselves, disobedient,
deceived, enslaved to various lusts and pleasures,
spending our life in malice and envy, hateful, hating one
another. But when the kindness of God our Savior and His
love for mankind appeared, He saved us, not on the basis
of deeds which we have done in righteousness, but
according to His mercy, by the washing of regeneration and
renewing by the Holy Spirit.

TITUS 3:3–5

THE SAME FALSE BELIEF *(I MUST MEET CERTAIN STANDARDS TO feel good about myself)* that drives people to perfectionism also sends them into a tailspin of despair. They rarely expect to achieve anything or to feel good about themselves. Because of their past failures, they are quick to interpret present failures as an accurate reflection of their worthlessness. Fearing more failure, they often become despondent and stop trying.

The pressure of having to meet self-imposed standards in order to feel good about ourselves can result in a rules-dominated life. Individuals caught in this trap often have a set of rules for most of life's situations, and continually focus their attention on their performance and ability to adhere to their schedule. Brent, for example, made a daily list of what he could accomplish if everything went perfectly. He was always a little tense because he wanted to use every moment effectively to reach his goals. If things didn't go well, or if someone took too much of his time, Brent got angry. Efficient, effective use of time was his way of attaining fulfillment, but he was miserable. He was constantly driven to do more, but his best was never enough to satisfy him.

- Do you have to be successful in order to feel good about yourself? What would you have to be or do to feel like you are a "success"?

- In what area(s) would you *never* allow yourself to fail?

As I reflect on how I feel so driven to perform, to meet the standards of others, Jesus, I admit . . .

DAY 19 _____

SETTLED ACCOUNTS

He made Him (Christ) who knew no sin to be sin on our behalf, that we might become the righteousness of God in Him.

2 CORINTHIANS 5:21

VISUALIZE TWO LEDGERS: ON ONE IS A LIST OF ALL YOUR SINS; ON the other, the righteousness of Christ. Now exchange your ledger for Christ's. This exemplifies justification— transferring our sin to Christ and His righteousness to us.

I once heard a radio preacher berate his congregation for their hidden sins. He exclaimed, "Don't you know that someday you're going to die and God is going to flash all your sins upon a giant screen in heaven for all the world to see?" How tragically this minister misunderstood God's gracious gift of justification!

Justification carries no guilt with it, and has no memory of past transgressions. Christ paid for all of our sins at the cross—past, present, and future. Hebrews 10:17 says, *And their sins and their lawless deeds I will remember no more.* We are completely forgiven by God!

_____

- Why did you need to be justified and have Christ's righteousness attributed to you?

Father, thank You for . . .

DAY 20 _____

MOTIVATIONS FOR OBEDIENCE

Therefore having been justified by faith, we have peace
with God through our Lord Jesus Christ.

ROMANS 5:1

SOME PEOPLE HAVE DIFFICULTY THINKING OF THEMSELVES AS
being pleasing to God because they link *pleasing* so
strongly with performance. They tend to be displeased
with anything short of perfection in themselves, and
suspect that God has the same standard.

The point of justification is that we can never achieve
perfection on this earth; even our best efforts at self-
righteousness are as filthy rags to God (Isaiah 64:6). Yet,
He loves us so much that He appointed His Son to pay for
our sins and give to us His own righteousness, His perfect
status before God.

This doesn't mean that our actions are irrelevant,
and that we can sin all we want. Our sinful actions,
words, and attitudes grieve the Lord, but our status as
beloved children remains intact. In His love, He disciplines
and encourages us to live godly lives—both for our good
and for His honor.

The Apostle Paul was so enamored with his
forgiveness and righteousness in Christ that he was
intensely motivated to please God by his actions and his
deeds. In 1 Corinthians 6:19–20; 2 Corinthians 5:9;

47

Philippians 3:8–11, and in other passages, Paul strongly stated his desire to please, honor, and glorify the One who had made him righteous.

Some people may read these statements and become uneasy, believing that I am discounting the gravity of sin. As you will see, I am not minimizing the destructive nature of sin, but am simply trying to elevate our view of the results of Christ's payment on the cross. Understanding our complete forgiveness and acceptance before God does not promote a casual attitude toward sin. On the contrary, it gives us a greater desire to live for and serve the One who died to free us from sin.

- How does being justified and having Christ's righteousness lead you to the conclusion: *I am completely forgiven by God, and am fully pleasing to Him?*

God, as I reflect on the magnitude of Your forgiveness and unconditional love for me, I feel . . .

JOURNAL _____ WEEK 4

From my reflection this week, I learned . . .

    . . . about God.

    . . . about myself.

    . . . about my motivations.

One thing I want to apply is:

Lord, I hope . . .

Lord, I need you to . . .

Day 21_____

CHRIST'S LOVE

For the love of Christ controls us, having concluded this,
that one died for all, therefore all died; and He died for all,
that they who live should no longer live for themselves, but
for Him who died and rose again on their behalf.

2 CORINTHIANS 5:14–15

UNDERSTANDING GOD'S GRACE COMPELS US TO ACTION BECAUSE love motivates us to please the One who has so freely loved us. When we experience love, we usually respond by seeking to express our love in return. Our obedience to God is an expression of our love for Him (John 14:15, 21), which comes from an understanding of what Christ has accomplished for us on the cross (2 Corinthians 5:14–15). We love because He first loved us and clearly demonstrated His love for us at the cross (1 John 4:16–19). Understanding this will highly motivate us to serve Him.

This great motivating factor is missing in many of our lives because we don't really believe that God loves us unconditionally. We expect His love to be conditional, based on our ability to earn it.

Our experience of God's love is based on our perception. If we believe that He is demanding or aloof, we will not be able to receive His love and tenderness. Instead, we will either be afraid of Him or angry with

Him. Faulty perceptions of God often prompt us to rebel against Him.

Our image of God is the foundation for all of our motivations. As we grow in our understanding of His unconditional love and acceptance, we will be better able to grasp that His discipline is prompted by care, not cruelty. We will also be increasingly able to perceive the contrast between the joys of living for Christ and the destructive nature of sin. We will be motivated to experience eternal rewards *where neither moth nor rust destroys* (Matthew 6:20). And we will want our lives to bring honor to the One who loves us so much.

- Does the love of Christ compel you to obey Him? Why, or why not?

I will try to honor You today in my actions, words, and thoughts. As I grow in my awareness of just how much You care about me, Father, and how much I care about You, I realize that I cannot grieve You without grieving myself. I give thanks to You today for . . .

DAY 22_____

SIN IS DESTRUCTIVE

For the wages of sin is death, but the free gift of God is
eternal life in Christ Jesus our Lord.
ROMANS 6:23

SATAN HAS EFFECTIVELY BLINDED MAN TO THE PAINFUL,
damaging consequences of sin. The effects of sin are all
around us, yet many continue to indulge in the sex,
status- and pleasure-seeking, and rampant self-
centeredness that cause so much anguish and pain. Satan
contradicted God in the Garden when he said, *You surely
shall not die!* (Genesis 3:4). Sin is pleasant, but only for a
season. Sooner or later, sin will result in some form of
destruction.

Sin is destructive in many ways. Emotionally, we
may experience the pain of guilt and shame and the fear
of failure and punishment. Mentally, we may experience
the anguish of flashbacks. We may also expend enormous
amounts of time and energy thinking about our sins and
rationalizing our guilt. Physically, we may suffer from
psychosomatic illnesses or experience pain through
physical abuse. Sin may also result in the loss of property,
or even the loss of life. Relationally, we can alienate
ourselves from others. Spiritually, we grieve the Holy
Spirit, lose our testimony, and break our fellowship with
God. The painful and destructive effects of sin are so

profound that why we don't have an aversion to it is a mystery!

———————

• How can viewing sin as destructive be a motivation for obedience to God?

Looking at my own life, I can see the far-reaching effects of sin's destruction. I long to be more like who I really am in You, Lord. As we walk together today, I need You to . . .

Day 23 _____

THE FATHER'S DISCIPLINE

All discipline for the moment seems not to be joyful, but
sorrowful; yet to those who have been trained by it,
afterwards it yields the peaceful fruit of righteousness.
HEBREWS 12:11

OUR LOVING FATHER HAS GIVEN US THE HOLY SPIRIT TO CONVICT
us of sin. Conviction is a form of God's discipline, and
serves as proof that we have become sons of God (Hebrews
12:5–11). It warns us that we are making choices without
regard to either God's truth or sin's consequences. If we
choose to be unresponsive to the Holy Spirit, our heavenly
Father will discipline us in love. Many people do not
understand the difference between discipline and
punishment. The following chart shows their profound
contrasts:

	PUNISHMENT	DISCIPLINE
SOURCE:	God's Wrath	God's Love
PURPOSE:	To Avenge a Wrong	To Correct a Wrong
RELATIONAL RESULT:	Alienation	Reconciliation
PERSONAL RESULT:	Guilt	A Righteous Lifestyle
DIRECTED TOWARD:	Non-Believers	His Children

Jesus bore all the punishment we deserved on the
cross; therefore, we no longer need to fear punishment

55

from God for our sins. We should seek to do what is right so that our Father will not have to correct us through discipline, but when we are disciplined, we should remember that God is correcting us in love. This discipline leads us to righteous performance, a reflection of Christ's righteousness in us.

- Do you sometimes confuse God's correction with punishment? If so, why?

Heavenly Father, if there is sin in my life that I am denying, please convict me of it through the power of Your Holy Spirit . . .

DAY 24 _____

HIS COMMANDS FOR US ARE GOOD

Thy word is a lamp to my feet,
  And a light to my path.
I have sworn, and I will confirm it,
  That I will keep Thy righteous ordinances.
                    PSALMS 119:105–106

GOD'S COMMANDS ARE GIVEN FOR TWO GOOD PURPOSES: TO protect us from the destructiveness of sin, and to direct us in a life of joy and fruitfulness. We have a wrong perspective if we only view God's commands as restrictions in our lives. Instead, we must realize that His commands are guidelines, given so that we might enjoy life to the fullest. God's commands should never be considered as a means to gain His approval.

In today's society, we have lost the concept of doing something because it is the right thing to do. Instead, we do things in exchange for some reward or favor, or to avoid punishment. Wouldn't it be novel to do something simply because it is the right thing to do? God's commands are holy, right, and good, and the Holy Spirit gives us the wisdom and strength to keep them. Therefore, since they have value in themselves, we can choose to obey God and follow His commands.

_____

- How can viewing God's commands as good be a motivation to you?

Thank You for Your commands, dear Lord. I need to remember that they're not dead ends, blocking my path to happiness. Instead, they are sensible routes in the journey of my life when I'm wise enough to follow them. I trust You to . . .

DAY 25 _____

ETERNAL REWARDS

For we must all appear before the judgment seat of
Christ, that each one may be recompensed for his deeds in
the body, according to what he has done, whether good or
bad.

2 CORINTHIANS 5:10

Y ET ANOTHER COMPELLING REASON TO LIVE FOR GOD'S GLORY IS
the fact that we will be rewarded in heaven for our service
to Him.

Now if any man builds upon the foundation with gold,
silver, precious stones, wood, hay, straw, each man's work
will become evident; for the day will show it, because it is to
be revealed with fire; and the fire itself will test the quality of
each man's work. If any man's work which he has built
upon it remains, he shall receive a reward. If any man's
work is burned up, he shall suffer loss; but he himself shall
be saved, yet so as through fire.

1 CORINTHIANS 3:12–15

Through Christ's payment for us on the cross, we
have escaped eternal judgment; however, our actions will
be judged at the judgment seat of Christ. There, our
performance will be evaluated and rewards presented for
service to God. Rewards will be given for deeds that

59

reflect a desire to honor Christ, but deeds performed in an attempt to earn God's acceptance, earn the approval of others, or meet our own standards will be rejected by God and consumed by fire.

———————

• Read 1 Corinthians 9:24–27 and 2 Timothy 2:3–7; 4:7–8. How does receiving a reward become a motivation for obedience?

Thank You, God, for . . .

JOURNAL _____ WEEK 5

From my reflection this week, I learned . . .

. . . about God.

. . . about myself.

. . . about my motivations.

One thing I want to apply is:

Lord, I hope . . .

Lord, I need you to . . .

DAY 26 _____

CHRIST IS WORTHY

Whom have I in heaven but Thee?
   And besides Thee, I desire nothing on earth. . . .
But as for me, the nearness of God is my good;
   I have made the Lord God my refuge, that I may tell of
      all Thy works.

PSALM 73:25, 28

CHRIST IS WORTHY OF OUR AFFECTION AND OBEDIENCE. THERE is no other person, no goal, no fame or status, and no material possession that can compare with Him. The more we understand His love and majesty, the more we will praise Him and desire that He be honored at the expense of everything else.

   Our most noble motivation for serving Christ is simply that He is worthy of our love and obedience. The Apostle John recorded his vision of the Lord and his response to His glory:

   After these things I looked, and behold, a door standing open in heaven, and the first voice which I had heard, like the sound of a trumpet speaking with me, said, "Come up here, and I will show you what must take place after these things." Immediately I was in the Spirit; and behold, a throne was standing in heaven, and One sitting on the throne. And He who was sitting was like a jasper stone and a sardius in appearance; and there was a rainbow around the throne, like an emerald in appearance. And around the throne were twenty-four thrones; and upon the thrones I saw twenty-four elders sitting, clothed in white garments, and golden crowns on their heads. . . .

And when the living creatures give glory and honor and thanks to Him who sits on the throne, to Him who lives forever and ever, the twenty-four elders will fall down before Him who sits on the throne, and will worship Him who lives forever and ever, and will cast their crowns before the throne, saying,

"Worthy art Thou, our Lord and our God,
   to receive glory and honor and power;
for Thou didst create all things,
   and because of Thy will they existed,
   and were created."

REVELATION 4:1–4, 9–11

• How do you feel as you reflect on the passages from Revelation 4?

• Do they motivate you? Why, or why not?

Father, today I want to praise You for . . .

Day 27 _____

GIVING AND RECEIVING LOVE

"By this all men will know that you are My disciples, if
you have love for one another."
JOHN 13:35

A SYMPTOM OF OUR FEAR OF REJECTION IS OUR INABILITY TO
give and receive love. We find it difficult to open up and
reveal our inner thoughts and motives because we believe
that others will reject us if they know what we are really
like. Therefore, our fear of rejection leads us to superficial
relationships or isolation. The more we experience
isolation, the more we need acceptance. Psychologist Eric
Fromm once wrote, "The deep need of man is the need to
overcome separateness, to leave the prison of his
aloneness."

The fear of rejection is rampant, and loneliness is
one of the most dangerous and widespread problems in
America today. Some estimate that loneliness has already
reached epidemic proportions, and say that if it continues
to spread, it could seriously erode the emotional strength
of our country. Loneliness is not relegated only to
unbelievers. Ninety-two percent of the Christians
attending a recent Bible conference admitted in a survey
that feelings of loneliness were a major problem in their
lives. All shared a basic symptom: a sense of despair at
feeling unloved and a fear of being unwanted or
unaccepted.

65

For the most part, our modern society has responded inadequately to rejection and loneliness. Our response has been outer-directed, meaning that we try to copy the customs, dress, ideas, and behavioral patterns of a particular group, allowing the consensus of the group to determine what is correct for us. But conforming to a group will not fully provide the security we are so desperately seeking. Only God can provide that through His people, His Word, His Spirit, and His timing.

• How does the fear of being rejected (disapproved of) by people affect your life? Give examples:

Father, You made me a unique, special individual. Whenever I feel rejected by others, please hold me fast in the truth that You are satisfied with the results of Your work, and so shall I be content. Father, I trust You to . . .

DAY 28 _____

THE FEAR OF REJECTION

All who hate me whisper together against me;
    Against me they devise my hurt, saying,
"A wicked thing is poured out upon him,
    That when he lies down, he will not rise up again."
Even my close friend, in whom I trusted,
    Who ate my bread,
    Has lifted up his heel against me.
But Thou, O Lord, be gracious to me, and raise me up.
            PSALM 41:7–10A

VIRTUALLY ALL OF US FEAR REJECTION. WE CAN FALL PREY TO IT even when we've learned to harden our defenses in anticipation of someone's disapproval. Neither being defensive nor trying to please another person's every whim is the answer to this problem. These are only coping mechanisms which prevent us from dealing with the root of our fear.

Rejection is a type of communication. It conveys a message that someone else is unsatisfactory to us; that he or she doesn't measure up to a standard we've created or adopted. Sometimes, rejection is willfully used as an act of manipulation designed to control someone else. Usually, rejection is manifested by an outburst of anger, a disgusted look, an impatient answer, or a social snub. Whatever the form of behavior, it communicates disrespect, low value, and lack of appreciation. Nothing hurts quite like the message of rejection.

If this is true, why do we reject others so frequently? Again, rejection can be a very effective, though destructive, motivator. Without raising a finger, we can send the message that our targeted individual doesn't meet our standards. We can harness this person's instinctive desire for acceptance until we have changed and adapted his or her behavior to suit our tastes and purposes. This is how rejection enables us to control the actions of another human being.

- How have you used disapproval, silence, sarcasm, or criticism to get others to do what you wanted them to do?

Rejection is a powerful, destructive tool. Please remind me of this fact, Lord, as I relate to those around me today. Father, I hope . . .

DAY 29 _____

LIKE PUPPETS ON A STRING

For am I now seeking the favor of men, or of God? Or am I striving to please men? If I were still trying to please men, I would not be a bond-servant of Christ.

GALATIANS 1:10

How do you react to the fear of rejection? Some of us project a cool, impervious exterior, and consequently, never develop deep, satisfying relationships. Some of us are so fearful of rejection that we withdraw and decline almost everything, while others continually say yes to everyone, hoping to gain their approval. Some of us are shy and easily manipulated; some of us are sensitive to criticism and react defensively. A deep fear of rejection may prompt hostility and promote the development of nervous disorders.

Our fear of rejection will control us to the degree by which we base our self-worth on the opinions of others rather than on our relationship with God. Our dependence on others for value brings bondage, while abiding in the truths of Christ's love and acceptance brings freedom and joy.

_____

- Describe a situation when someone (friend, boss, parent, child) withheld approval, or used criticism, silence, sarcasm, or praise to manipulate you into doing what he or she wanted you to do. What did this person say or do? Did he or she succeed? Why, or why not?

When I think about what I just described, dear God, I feel a lot of different emotions. Please help me to sort them out, Lord, . . .

DAY 30 _____

CONDITIONAL APPROVAL

His speech was smoother than butter,
But his heart was war;
His words were softer than oil,
Yet they were drawn swords.
PSALM 55:21

MY DESIRE FOR THE APPROVAL OF OTHERS HAS OFTEN BEEN SO great that I sometimes joke about having been born an "approval addict." Growing up, I had the feeling that I didn't fit in; that I was "different" from others; that there was, therefore, something inherently wrong with me. I felt inadequate and tried to win the approval of others, desperately hoping that this would compensate for the negative feelings I had about myself.

But ironically, the conditional approval of others was never enough to satisfy me. Instead, being praised only reminded me of the disapproval I might encounter if I failed to maintain what I had achieved. I was thus compelled to work even harder at being successful. I occasionally find myself falling into this pattern of behavior even now, despite my improved knowledge, experience, and relationship with God.

———————

To see how others' expectations can affect you, answer the following:

- _____ would be more pleased with me if I would:

- _____ is proud of me when I:

- How does _____ attempt to get me to change by what he (or she) says and does?

- Things I do or say to get _____ to approve of me include:

Dear God, please help me to apply Your truths in my everyday life by . . .

JOURNAL _____ WEEK 6

From my reflection this week, I learned . . .

   . . . about God.

   . . . about myself.

   . . . about my motivations.

One thing I want to apply is:

Lord, I hope . . .

Lord, I need you to . . .

DAY 31_____

GOING DEEPER

I went about mourning
   as though it were my friend or brother;
I bowed down mourning,
   as one who sorrows for a mother.
But at my stumbling they rejoiced, and gathered
      themselves together;
   The smiters whom I did not know gathered together
      against me,
   They slandered me without ceasing.
                     PSALM 35:14–15

I DON'T BELIEVE THAT ANY OF US WILL GAIN COMPLETE FREEDOM from our propensity to base our self-worth on the approval of others until we see the Lord. Our God-given instinct to survive compels us to avoid pain. Knowing that rejection and disapproval bring pain, we will continue our attempts to win the esteem of others whenever possible. The good news is that because we are fully pleasing to God, we need not be devastated when others respond to us in a negative way.

As we grow in our relationship with God, the Holy Spirit will continue teaching us how to apply this liberating truth to different aspects of our lives at an increasingly deeper level. In fact, one evidence of His work within us is the ability to see new areas of our lives in which we are allowing the opinions of others to determine our sense of worth. With spiritual maturity, we will more often be able to identify these areas and choose to find our significance in God's unconditional love for us and complete acceptance of us. However, profound changes in our value system take honesty, objectivity, and prolonged, persistent application of God's Word.

———————

- Does spiritual growth lead to more complexity or more simplicity in your faith? Explain.

Father, as I grow in Your Word, please teach me more about . . .

Day 32_____

RECONCILIATION

And although you were formerly alienated and hostile in
mind, engaged in evil deeds, yet He has now reconciled
you in His fleshly body through death, in order to present
you before Him holy and blameless and beyond reproach.
COLOSSIANS 1:21–22

As I TALKED WITH Pam, IT BECAME OBVIOUS THAT SHE DID NOT
understand this great truth of reconciliation. Three years
after she married, Pam had committed adultery with a
coworker. Although she had confessed her sin to God and
to her husband, and had been forgiven, guilt continued to
plague her, making it difficult for her to feel acceptable to
God. Four years after the affair, she still could not forgive
herself for what she had done.

Sitting in my office, we explored her reluctance to
accept God's forgiveness.

"It sounds as though you believe that God can't
forgive the sin you committed," I said.

"That's right," she replied. "I don't think He ever
will."

"But God doesn't base His love and acceptance of us
on our performance," I said. "If any sin is so filthy and vile
that it makes us less acceptable to Him, then the cross is
insufficient. If the cross isn't sufficient for all sin, then
the Bible is in error when it says that He forgave *all* your

sins (Colossians 2:13–15). God took our sins and cancelled them by nailing them to Christ's cross. In this way, God also took away Satan's power to condemn us for sin. So you see, nothing you will ever do can nullify your reconciliation and make you unacceptable to God."

Our unconditional acceptance in Christ is a profound, life-changing truth. Salvation is not simply a ticket to heaven. It is the beginning of a dynamic new relationship with God. *Justification* is the doctrine that explains the judicial facts of our forgiveness and righteousness in Christ. *Reconciliation* explains the relational aspect of our salvation. The moment we receive Christ by faith, we enter into a personal relationship with Him. We are united with God in an eternal and inseparable bond (Romans 8:38–39). We are bound in an indissoluble union with Him, as fellow heirs with Christ. The Holy Spirit has sealed us in that relationship, and we are absolutely secure in Christ.

• Read Colossians 1:21–22. Compare your former state to your present condition:

Lord, I trust You to . . .

DAY 33 _____

DECLARED ACCEPTABLE

Having also believed, you were sealed in Him with the
Holy Spirit of promise, who is given as a pledge of our
inheritance, with a view to the redemption of God's own
possession, to the praise of His glory.

EPHESIANS 1:13–14

RECENTLY, IN A GROUP PRAYER MEETING, SOMEONE PRAYED,
"Thank you, God, for accepting me when I am so
unacceptable." This person understood that we cannot
earn God's acceptance by our own merit, but seemed to
have forgotten that we are unconditionally accepted in
Christ. We are no longer unacceptable—the point of the
cross. Through Christ's death and resurrection, we have
become acceptable to God. This did not occur because God
decided He could overlook our sin, but because Christ
forgave all of our sins so that He could present us to the
Father, holy and blameless.

Because of reconciliation, we are completely
acceptable to God and are completely accepted by God. As
these passages illustrate, we enjoy a full and complete
relationship with Him, and in this relationship, His
determination of our value is not based on our
performance.

———

- What is wrong with the statement, "Thank you, Lord, for accepting me even though I am so unacceptable"?

Sometimes it's hard to comprehend that I have been accepted by You, and that, because of Christ, I really am acceptable to You, Father.
Thank You, for . . .

DAY 34 _____

THE FINAL AUTHORITY

And in Him you have been made complete, and He is
the head over all rule and authority.
COLOSSIANS 2:10

W E CAN DO NOTHING TO CONTRIBUTE TO CHRIST'S FREE GIFT OF
salvation; furthermore, if we base our self-worth on the
approval of others, then we are actually saying that our
ability to please others is of greater value than Christ's
payment. We are the sinners, the depraved, the wretched,
and the helpless. He is the loving Father, the seeking,
searching, patient Savior who has made atonement for
the lost, and has extended to us His grace and sonship.
We add nothing to our salvation. It is God who seeks us
out, convicts us of sin, and reveals Himself to us. It is God
who gives us the very faith with which to accept Him. Our
faith is simply our response to what He has done for us.

So then, our worth lies in the fact that Christ's blood
has paid for our sins; therefore, we are reconciled to God.
We are accepted on that basis alone, but does this great
truth indicate that we don't need other people in our
lives? On the contrary, God very often uses other believers
to demonstrate His love and acceptance to us. The
strength, comfort, encouragement, and love of Christians
toward one another is a visible expression of God's love.
However, our acceptance and worth are not *dependent* on

others' acceptance of us, even if they are fellow believers! Whether they accept us or not, we are *still* deeply loved, completely forgiven, fully pleasing, totally accepted, and complete in Christ. *He alone* is the final authority on our worth and acceptance.

———————

• If you are completely and fully accepted by the perfect Creator of the universe, why do you fear the rejection of men?

Heavenly Father, please help me to understand how the fear of not being accepted has affected my life. Please show me . . .

DAY 35 _____

THE ROLE OF RELATIONSHIPS

Fathers, do not exasperate your children, that they may not lose heart.

COLOSSIANS 3:21

FOR MANY OF US, THE UNCONDITIONAL LOVE, FORGIVENESS, AND acceptance of Christ seems abstract, and is difficult to comprehend. We may understand the premise of these character traits, but may still be unable to incorporate them into our personal experience. Often, we can trace this difficulty to our parental relationships.

God intends for parents to model His character to their children. According to Scripture, parents are to give their children affection, compassion, protection, provision, and loving discipline. When parents provide this kind of environment in their home, children are usually able to transfer these perceptions to the character of God, and believe that He is loving, compassionate, protective, gracious, and a loving disciplinarian. In turn, they are often able to model these characteristics to their own children.

Many of us, however, have not received this parental model of God's character. On an extremely wide spectrum, some of us have had relatively healthy relationships with our parents, while others have experienced various forms of neglect, condemnation, and manipulation. Still others

83

have suffered the deeper wounds of sexual abuse, physical abuse, or abandonment. The greater the degree of dysfunction (or poor modeling) in a family, the greater the potential for emotional, spiritual, and relational wounds. Put another way, the poorer the parental modeling of God's love, forgiveness, and power, the greater our difficulty in experiencing and applying these characteristics in our lives.

––––––––––

• In what ways did your parents accurately reflect God's care, protection, and provision?

• In what ways did they misrepresent God's nature to you?

Father, please open my heart and my eyes so I may see how Your character differs from what I've seen modeled in my childhood. This may take a lot of honesty and objectivity on my part, but I want to grow closer to You, and I want to be a good role-model for my children (future children). I know I can trust You to . . .

JOURNAL _____ WEEK 7

From my reflection this week, I learned . . .

. . . about God.

. . . about myself.

. . . about my motivations.

One thing I want to apply is:

Lord, I hope . . .

Lord, I need you to . . .

DAY 36_____

HEALTHY VS. UNHEALTHY RELATIONSHIPS

Bear one another's burdens, and thus fulfill the law of Christ.

For each one shall bear his own load.

GALATIANS 6:2, 5

BECAUSE MANY OF US ARE SO VULNERABLE WHEN WE BEGIN allowing ourselves to experience the pain that usually accompanies growth, it is wise to have a basic understanding of healthy and unhealthy relationships.

We must first understand that while God often demonstrates His love and affirmation for us through believers and non-believers alike, His desire is that our relationships with others will enable us to know Him more fully. His work through others is, in part, to serve as a channel by which we can better understand His divine love and acceptance of us. Sadly, we are all prone to miss His message and mistake His messenger(s) as the source of our fulfillment. When this misperception is carried to an extreme, we can fall into *emotional dependency*, "the condition resulting when the ongoing presence and/or nurturing of another is believed necessary for personal security."*

In his book, *The Four Loves*, C. S. Lewis described the difference between lovers and friends:

* Lori Thorkelson Rentzel, *Emotional Dependency* (San Rafael, CA: Exodus International America, Box 2121, 94912).

Lovers are always talking to one another about their
love; Friends hardly ever about their Friendship. Lovers are
normally face to face, absorbed in each other; Friends, side
by side, absorbed in some common interest. Above all,
Eros (while it lasts) is necessary between two only. But two,
far from being the necessary number for Friendship, is not
even the best.*

Healthy relationships are turned outward, rather
than inward. Healthy relationships encourage
individuality rather than conformity, and are concerned
with independence, rather than emotional dependence.
Healthy relationships point one's focus to the Lord and
pleasing Him, rather than toward the friendship and
pleasing one another.

———————

• What are some characteristics of healthy relationships?
  Of unhealthy ones?

*It's good to have a basic understanding of healthy
and unhealthy relationships. Lord, I look to You for
discernment as I apply what I'm learning to my
present and future relationships. Please cross my
path with fellow Christians who are seeking healthy
friendships. Thank You for . . .*

* C. S. Lewis, *The Four Loves* (New York: Harcourt Brace Jovanovich,
Inc., 1960), pp. 91–92,

Day 37 _____

AVOIDING EMOTIONAL DEPENDENCY

Therefore, laying aside falsehood, speak truth, each one of you, with his neighbor, for we are members of one another.

EPHESIANS 4:25

How do we know when we've crossed the line from a healthy relationship to one that is emotionally dependent? When either party in a relationship:*

- experiences frequent jealousy, possessiveness and a desire for exclusivism, viewing other people as a threat to the relationship.
- prefers to spend time alone with this friend and becomes frustrated when this does not happen.
- becomes irrationally angry or depressed when this friend withdraws slightly.
- loses interest in a friendship other than this one.
- experiences romantic or sexual feelings leading to fantasy about this person.
- becomes preoccupied by the person's appearance, personality, problems, and interests.
- is unwilling to make short- or long-range plans that do not include the other person.

*Lori Thorkelson Rentzel, *Emotional Dependency*, pp. 3–4. Reprinted by permission.

- is unable to see the other's faults realistically.
- becomes defensive about this relationship when asked about it.
- displays physical affection beyond what is appropriate for a friendship.
- refers frequently to the other in conversation; feels free to "speak for" the other.
- exhibits an intimacy and familiarity with this friend that causes others to feel uncomfortable or embarrassed in their presence.

Our relationships with one another are very important to God; so much so, that He has placed unity among the brethren as a priority in our relationship with Him (see Matthew 5:23–24). This is because God has reconciled us to Himself as a *body* in Christ (Ephesians 2:16), and therefore intends for us to interact as *members of one another* (Ephesians 4:25).

Pray that God will guide you to relationships which will encourage you to be honest; practice the truth of His Word; affirm you, and thereby help you develop an appropriate love for yourself; and compel you to focus on Him as the gracious provider of your needs. Eventually, your gratitude will motivate you to practice pleasing Him rather than other people.

- Do any of the characteristics of dependent relationships apply to your relationships? Which ones? What can you do about them?

Thank You for everything I've learned about dependent relationships, Lord. As I think about my friends, family, coworkers, and other relationships, please show me which ones I need to recognize as being emotionally dependent upon me or those upon which I am emotionally dependent. Lord, I trust You to . . .

DAY 38 _____

THE FATHER'S LOVE

If I speak with the tongues of men and of angels, but do not have love, I have become a noisy gong or a clanging cymbal. And if I have the gift of prophecy, and know all mysteries and all knowledge; and if I have all faith, so as to remove mountains, but do not have love, I am nothing.

1 CORINTHIANS 13:1–2

HOW DO WE LEARN TO REJECT SATAN'S LIE, *I MUST BE APPROVED by certain others to feel good about myself*? How can we begin to practically apply the great truth of our reconciliation to Almighty God? The following exercise will help you begin to experience the freedom and joy of reconciliation.

The thirteenth chapter of First Corinthians describes God's unconditional love and acceptance of us. To personalize this passage, replace the word *love* with *My Father*. Then, memorize the following, and when fear comes to you, recall the love and kindness of God:

My Father is very patient and kind.
My Father is not envious, never boastful.
My Father is not arrogant.
My Father is never rude, nor is He self-seeking.
My Father is not quick to take offense.
My Father keeps no score of wrongs.

My Father does not gloat over my sins, but is always glad when truth prevails.
My Father knows no limit to His endurance, no end to His trust.
My Father is always hopeful and patient.

As you memorize this passage, ask God to show you if your perception of Him is in error in any way. This will enable you to have a more accurate perception of God, and will help you to experience more of His unconditional love and acceptance.

———————

• Describe your thoughts and feelings as you reflect on the paraphrase of 1 Corinthians 13:

When I read the thirteenth chapter of 1 Corinthians, I feel humbled, overwhelmed, grateful, joyful ... Your Spirit fills me with love, compassion, reverence, patience ...

DAY 39 _____

ASSIGNING BLAME

And so, as those who have been chosen of God, holy and beloved, put on a heart of compassion, kindness, humility, gentleness and patience; bearing with one another, and forgiving each other, whoever has a complaint against anyone, just as the Lord forgave you, so also should you.

COLOSSIANS 3:12–13

WHETHER CONSCIOUSLY OR UNCONSCIOUSLY, WE ALL TEND TO point an accusing finger, assigning blame for virtually every failure. Whenever we fail to receive approval for our performance, we are likely to search for a reason, a culprit, a scapegoat. More often than not, we can find no one but ourselves to blame, so the accusing finger points right back at us. Self-condemnation is a severe form of punishment.

If possible, we will often try to place the blame on others and fulfill the law of retribution—that people should get what they deserve. For most of our lives, we have been conditioned to make someone pay for failures or shortcomings. When we miss a deadline at work because we didn't use our time wisely and don't want to admit it, we try to find someone else to take the blame. When a problem is partly our fault and partly someone else's, we often are quick to mention the other person's culpability.

For every flaw we see around us, we often search for someone to blame. Some of us internalize, blaming ourselves for everything and anything that anybody did wrong. Others externalize the blame, hoping to exonerate ourselves by making sure others are identified as "guilty" and punished.

———————

• Does condemning yourself help you become a better person? Why, or why not?

Heavenly Father, today I will try not to be so hard on myself and others. As I look to You for a model of compassion, please show me . . .

DAY 40 _____

DEFENDING AND BLAMING

But if you bite and devour one another, take care lest
you be consumed by one another. But I say, walk by the
Spirit and you will not carry out the desire of the flesh.
GALATIANS 5:15–16

ANOTHER REASON WE SEEK TO BLAME OTHERS IS THAT OUR
success often depends on their contributions. Their failures
are threats to us. When these failures block our goals of
success, we usually respond by defending ourselves and
blaming others, often using condemnation to manipulate
them to improve their performance. Blaming others also
helps put a safe distance between their failures and our
fragile self-worth.

Whether our accusations are focused on ourselves or
others, we all have a tendency to believe that someone
has to take the blame. When Ellen discovered that her
fifteen-year-old daughter was pregnant, she went a week
without sleep, tossing and turning, trying to determine
who was at fault. Was it her daughter, who had brought
this reproach on the family, or was she to blame for
failing as a mother? All Ellen knew was that someone had
to take responsibility for the crisis.

Rather than being objective and looking for a solid,
biblical solution to our problems, we often resort to either
accusing someone else or berating ourselves.

_____

- Think of a close friend or family member with whom you've had a conflict. What did you say or do to inflict emotional pain?

- What are some reasons you said or did those things?

*Lord, I've said and done some things that have hurt
_____ . There was a better way of
handling my emotions and I admit . . .*

JOURNAL _____ WEEK 8

From my reflection this week, I learned . . .

. . . about God.

. . . about myself.

. . . about my motivations.

One thing I want to apply is:

Lord, I hope . . .

Lord, I need you to . . .

DAY 41 _____

ONE UP—ONE DOWN

Therefore consider the members of your earthly body as dead to immorality, impurity, passion, evil desire, and greed, which amounts to idolatry. For it is on account of these things that the wrath of God will come, and in them you also once walked, when you were living in them. But now you also, put them all aside: anger, wrath, malice, slander, and abusive speech from your mouth.

COLOSSIANS 3:5–8

SOMETIMES, WE BLAME OTHERS TO MAKE OURSELVES FEEL BETTER. By blaming someone else who failed, we feel superior. In fact, the higher the position of the one who failed (parent, boss, pastor, etc.), the farther they fall, and often, the better we feel. This desire to be superior, to be "one up" on someone, is at the root of gossip.

In other situations, however, just the opposite is true. When a parent fails, a child usually accepts the blame for that failure. Even as adults, we may readily assume blame in our relationships with those in authority. We have much invested in supporting those we depend upon. This is one reason why denial is so strong in abusive families. For example, one little girl said, "I never told anybody that Daddy was molesting me because I thought that somebody would take him away from our family."

- Describe three recent incidents in your life in which
  you feared being blamed or punished. Why did you
  have this fear?

*Jesus, it's not easy to stand up and accept the full
responsibility of my wrongdoings. I am comforted,
though, by knowing that You are pleased by my
efforts to do so. Thank You for . . .*

DAY 42 _____

RESPONDING TO OTHERS' FAILURES

And be kind to one another, tender-hearted, forgiving each other, just as God in Christ also has forgiven you.

EPHESIANS 4:32

How should we respond when another fails? If the person who failed is a Christian, we need to affirm God's truth about him or her: *He(or she) is deeply loved, completely forgiven, fully pleasing, and totally accepted by God, and complete in Christ.* This perspective can eventually change our condemning attitude to one of love and a desire to help. By believing these truths, we will gradually be able to love this person just as God loves us (1 John 4:11), forgive him or her just as God has forgiven us (Ephesians 4:32), and accept him or her just as God has accepted us (Romans 15:7). This does not mean that we will become blind to the faults or failures of others. We will continue to see them, but our response to them will change considerably over time, from condemnation to compassion. As we depend less on other people for our self-worth, their sins and mistakes will become less of a threat to us, and we will desire to help them instead of being compelled to punish them.

- How do you normally respond to other Christians' sins and failures?

- How would you like to respond now?

Heavenly Father, teach me Your way of compassion. Please show me . . .

DAY 43 _____

CONDEMNING PEOPLE FOR MISTAKES

Never pay back evil for evil to anyone. Respect what is right in the sight of all men.

If possible, so far as it depends on you, be at peace with all men.

ROMANS 12:17–18

WE TEND TO MAKE TWO MAJOR ERRORS WHEN WE PUNISH others for their failures. The first is that we condemn people not only for genuine sin, but also for their mistakes. When people who have tried their best fail, they do not need our biting blame. They need our love and encouragement. Again, we often tend to blame others because their actions (whether they reflect overt disobedience or honest mistakes) make us look like failures, and our own failure is unacceptable to us. Husband-wife, parent-child, and employer-employee relationships are especially vulnerable to one's being threatened by the failure of another. A wife gets angry with her husband for his not-so-funny joke at an important dinner party; a parent erupts at a child for accidentally spilling milk; a manager scowls at an employee because an error in the employee's calculations has made him look foolish to his supervisor. People generally experience difficulty in dealing with their *sins*; let's not compound their problems by condemning them for their *mistakes*.

104

A second major error we often make by condemning others is believing that we are godly agents of condemnation. Unable to tolerate injustice, we seem to possess a great need to balance the scales of right and wrong. We are correct in recognizing that sin is reprehensible and deserves condemnation; yet, we have not been licensed by God to punish others for their sins. Judgment is God's responsibility, not man's.

Jesus dealt specifically with this issue when several men decided to stone a woman caught in adultery. He told them that the person without sin should throw the first stone. Beginning with the eldest, all of the accusers walked away as they remembered their own sins (John 8:3–9). In light of their own sinfulness, they no longer saw fit to condemn the sins of another.

As this incident clearly illustrates, we should leave righteous condemnation and punishment in the hands of the One worthy of the responsibility. Our response should be love, affirmation, and possibly, compassionate correction.

———————

- Which of these errors do you tend to make?

- How does that affect you? Your relationships?

Dear Lord, please give me the desire to encourage and build up others rather than condemn and punish them. Help me remember that "treating others how I would like to be treated" includes my responses to their mistakes and failures, too. Please let me sense Your nearness today as ...

Day 44_____

PRIVILEGES OF SONSHIP

"You are of your father the devil," Jesus explained, "and
you want to do the desires of your father."
JOHN 8:44

WORDS LIKE THESE MAKE IT EASY FOR US TO UNDERSTAND WHY
we believe Satan's lies so readily!

However, at some point in our lives, the Holy Spirit
drew us to Christ, and we trusted Him to forgive us and
give us new purpose and meaning in our existence. The
Holy Spirit baptized us into the body of Christ, a new
spiritual family, the family of God. He plucked us from
the family of Satan (Colossians 1:13–14) and adopted us
into God's eternal family as sons and daughters (Romans
8:15). We were cursed to die as members of Satan's family,
but as members of God's family, we were granted
everything pertaining to life and godliness at the very
moment of our new birth. We were not forced to qualify to
receive God's provisions, but instead have received the
rights and privileges of sons by His grace and mercy.

In one of the most famous dialogues in the Bible, Jesus
explained the profound truth of regeneration to Nicodemus:
". . . unless one is born again, he cannot see the kingdom of God . . . . That which is born of the flesh is flesh,
and that which is born of the Spirit is spirit. Do not marvel
that I said to you, 'You must be born again.'"
JOHN 3:3, 6–7

- What does "grace" mean to you?

- How has your understanding of God's attitude toward you changed?

Heavenly Father, thank You for . . .

DAY 45 _____

HONEST OR NOT?

A prudent man conceals knowledge,
But the heart of fools proclaims folly.
PROVERBS 12:23

WHEN OTHERS OFFEND OR INSULT US, SHOULD WE TELL THEM that they have made us angry or hurt our feelings? This question can be difficult to answer. Some psychologists tell us that we should vent all of our emotions because repression is unhealthy. Others tell us that our emotions will always be positive and controlled if we are truly walking with the Lord. We should avoid both of these extremes. Venting our anger uncontrollably is not a healthy solution, but neither is continued repression and denial.

We need a safe environment to express our emotions: a good friend or counselor who will help us get in touch with our true feelings, which we may have suppressed for years. We can also learn to express ourselves fully to the Lord and tell Him our true feelings, fears, hopes, and dreams. (The Psalms are filled with honest expressions of anger, pain, confusion, hope, and faith.) In this safe environment, we can slowly learn how to communicate appropriately with those who have hurt us. This requires wisdom because each situation and each person often requires a different form of communication.

- What factors determine how, if, how much, and when you tell someone of your hurt and anger? Who can you talk to honestly about your pain?

Christ Jesus, I don't want to run away from my emotions, and, likewise, I don't want to express myself to others who have offended me in such a way that I end up offending them. Please help me to pause long enough to assess a situation and seek Your wisdom in how to respond. I need You to . . .

JOURNAL _____WEEK 9

From my reflection this week, I learned . . .

   . . . about God.

   . . . about myself.

   . . . about my motivations.

One thing I want to apply is:

Lord, I hope . . .

Lord, I need you to . . .

Day 46 _____

A HEALTHY SENSE OF ASSERTIVENESS

But speaking the truth in love, we are to grow up in all aspects into Him, who is the head, even Christ.
EPHESIANS 4:15

As WE LEARN TO RELATE APPROPRIATELY WITH THOSE WHO HAVE hurt or injured us in some way, we will begin to develop a healthy sense of assertiveness—an important component in shaping other people's behavior toward us. For example, if others are rude, but never realize it because we passively accept their behavior in an attempt to avoid upsetting them, at least two things usually happen: We develop resentment toward them, and they never have to come to terms with their negative impact on others. They then miss an important opportunity to change, and we effectually prolong their hurtful behavior. There are appropriate and inappropriate ways of communicating our sense of anger or resentment to others, but these feelings need to be spoken—for their benefit and for ours.

We also need to remember that learning how to express our feelings appropriately is a *process*. We can't expect to respond perfectly to everyone. It takes time to express years of repressed pain. It also takes time to learn how to respond firmly and clearly. Be patient with yourself.

113

We have a choice in our response to failure: We can condemn or we can learn. All of us fail, but this doesn't mean that we are failures. We need to understand that failing can be a step toward maturity, not a permanent blot on our self-esteem. Like children first learning to walk, we all stumble and fall. And, just like children, we can pick ourselves up and begin again. We don't have to allow failure to prevent us from being used by God.

• Describe a "healthy sense of assertiveness."

• How much is too much? How much is too little?

Lord, as I learn how to respond to others in a proper, assertive way, please give me discernment, patience, and . . .

DAY 47 _____

INORDINATE FEAR OF GOD

For we do not have a high priest who is unable to sympathize with our weaknesses, but we have one who has been tempted in every way, just as we are—yet was without sin. Let us then approach the throne of grace with confidence, so that we may receive mercy and find grace to help us in our time of need.

HEBREWS 4:15–16, NIV

THERE HAVE BEEN MANY TIMES IN MY LIFE WHEN I FELT THAT God was going to punish me by causing me to lose all that I had, either because I'd done something I shouldn't have, or because I'd failed to do something I should have. This erroneous perception of God has driven me away from Him on many occasions when I've needed Him most, and is completely contrary to the One whom Paul described as *the Father of mercies and God of all comfort* (2 Corinthians 1:3).

If we have trusted Christ for our salvation, God has forgiven us, and wants us to experience His forgiveness on a daily basis. Moses was a murderer, but God forgave him and used him to deliver Israel from Egypt. David was an adulterer and a murderer, but God forgave him and made him a great king. Peter denied the Lord, but God forgave him, and Peter became a leader in the Church. God rejoices when His children learn to accept His

115

forgiveness, pick themselves up, and walk after they have stumbled. But we must also learn to forgive ourselves. Rather than viewing our weaknesses as a threat to our self-esteem, it is God's desire that they compel us to move forward in our relationship with Him.

• What are some reasons we may have an inordinate fear of God?

• What are some differences between a healthy respect to God and this inordinate fear?

*Father, I will remind myself every morning that I have been forgiven by You. And because **You** have forgiven me, I can forgive myself . . .*

DAY 48 _____

FOR WHOM DID CHRIST DIE?

For while we were still helpless, at the right time Christ
died for the ungodly. For one will hardly die for a righteous
man; though perhaps for the good man someone would
dare even to die. But God demonstrates His own love
toward us, in that while we were yet sinners, Christ died for
us.

ROMANS 5:6–8

To UNDERSTAND GOD'S WONDROUS PROVISION OF PROPITIATION,
it is helpful to remember what He has endured from
mankind. From Adam and Eve's sin in the Garden of
Eden to the obvious depravity we see in our world today,
human history is mainly the story of greed, hatred, lust,
and pride—evidence of man's wanton rebellion against
the God of love and peace. If not done with a desire to
glorify Him, even our "good" deeds are like filthy garments
to God (Isaiah 64:6).

Our sin deserves the righteous wrath of God. He is
the Almighty, the rightful judge of the universe. He is
absolutely holy and perfect. *God is light, and in Him there
is no darkness at all* (1 John 1:5). Because of these
attributes, God cannot overlook sin, nor can He
compromise by accepting sinful behavior. For God to
condone even one sin would defile His holiness like
smearing a white satin wedding gown with black tar.

117

Because He is holy, God's aversion to sin is manifested in righteous anger. However, God is not only righteously indignant about sin, He is also infinitely loving. In His holiness, God condemns sin, but in the most awesome example of love the world has ever seen, He ordained that His Son would die to pay for our sins. God sacrificed the sinless, perfect Savior to turn away, *to propitiate,* His great wrath.

And for whom did Christ die? Was it for the saints who honored Him? Was it for a world that appreciated His sinless life and worshipped Him? No! Christ died for *us,* while we were yet in rebellion against Him.

- Why is it significant to realize that Christ died for you personally and not only for "all people"? How does that make you feel?

Heavenly Father, thank You for . . .

DAY 49 _____

THE FATHOMLESS LOVE OF CHRIST

For I am convinced that neither death, nor life, nor angels, nor principalities, nor things present, nor things to come, nor powers, nor height, nor depth, nor any other created thing, shall be able to separate us from the love of God, which is in Christ Jesus our Lord.

ROMANS 8:38–39

WHO CAN MEASURE THE FATHOMLESS DEPTH OF LOVE THAT sent Christ to the cross? While we were the enemies of God, Christ averted the wrath we deserved so that we might become the sons of God.

What can we say of our holy heavenly Father? Surely, He did not escape seeing Christ's mistreatment at the hands of sinful men—the scourgings, the humiliation, the beatings. Surely, He who spoke the world into being could have delivered Christ from the entire ordeal. And yet, the God of heaven peered down through time and saw you and me. Though we were His enemies, He loved us and longed to rescue us from our sins, and designated the sinless Christ to become our substitute. Only Christ could avert God's righteous wrath against sin, so in love, the Father kept silent as Jesus hung from the cross. All of His anger, all of the wrath we would ever deserve, was poured

119

upon Christ, and Christ became sin for us (2 Corinthians 5:21). Because he paid the penalty for our sins, and God's wrath was avenged, God no longer looks upon us through the eyes of judgment, but instead, He now lavishes His love upon us. The Scriptures teach that absolutely nothing can separate us from God's love (Romans 8:38–39). He has adopted us into a tender, intimate, and powerful relationship with Him (Romans 8:15).

• What does it mean to "lavish love" on someone?

• Do you sense that God lavishes His love on you? Why or why not?

Thank You, God, for the love that you lavish on me. I feel . . .

Day 50_____

LETTING GO

That, in reference to your former manner of life, you lay aside the old self, which is being corrupted in accordance with the lusts of deceit, and that you be renewed in the spirit of your mind, and put on the new self, which in the likeness of God has been created in righteousness and holiness of the truth.

EPHESIANS 4:22–24

TOO OFTEN, OUR SELF-IMAGE RESTS SOLELY ON AN EVALUATION of our past behavior, being measured only through a memory. Day after day, year after year, we tend to build our personalities upon the rubble of yesterday's personal disappointments.

Perhaps we find some strange kind of comfort in our personal failings. Perhaps there is some security in accepting ourselves as much less than we can become. That minimizes the risk of failure. Certainly, if we expect little from ourselves we will seldom be disappointed!

But nothing forces us to remain in the mold of the past. By the grace and power of God, we can change! We can persevere and overcome! No one forces us to keep shifting our feet in the muck of old failures. We can dare to accept the challenge of building a new life.

Dr. Paul Tournier once compared life to a man hanging from a trapeze. The trapeze bar was the man's

121

security, his pattern of existence, his lifestyle. Then God swung another trapeze into the man's view, and he faced a perplexing dilemma. Should he relinquish his past? Should he reach for the new bar? The moment of truth came, Dr. Tournier explained, when the man realized that to grab onto the new bar, he must release the old one.

• What memories and wounds of the past enslave you?

• How can you let them go and build a new identity, new qualities in relationships, and a new hope?

• What sources of input reinforce a low view of yourself?

Jesus, the past has left some scars on me. Some of them are small, others are quite apparent. You know my wounds, You know my needs. It's not always easy to let go of the past, but I realize I must if You are going to be in control of my present and my future . . .

JOURNAL _____ WEEK 10

From my reflection this week, I learned . . .

. . . about God.

. . . about myself.

. . . about my motivations.

One thing I want to apply is:

Lord, I hope . . .

Lord, I need you to . . .

DAY 51_____

GRASPING GOD'S VIEW

I can do all things through Him who strengthens me.
PHILIPPIANS 4:13

OUR PAST RELATIONSHIPS MAY INVOLVE THE INTENSE PAIN OF neglect, abuse, and manipulation, but if we do not begin the process of healing, we will be unable to experience the joy, challenge, and yes, the potential for failure in the present.

I have struggled with this process of change for the greater part of my life. It may have been that I was raised in a poor family. It may have been that while I was growing up, I often felt very awkward. It may have been that there were some inadequacies in my home life. For whatever reasons, I grew up with a sense of shame about myself and my circumstances.

I often felt inadequate during my childhood. I had the impression that I just didn't measure up. Others might not have thought I felt this way, but my sense of inadequacy was often intense.

Being exceptionally tall and lanky, I was uncomfortable with the way I looked, and felt out of place among my peers. My feelings of inferiority prevented me from pursuing dating relationships for a number of years. The threat of potential rejection prompted me to withdraw from social gatherings, preferring instead to spend time with the few friends I felt most comfortable with.

The truth that I am deeply loved, fully pleasing, and totally accepted by the God of the universe has taken me a lifetime to comprehend. But gradually, by studying God's Word and by experiencing loving relationships with other believers who genuinely care for me and appreciate me, I have continued to gain a better understanding of the way God values me. This has improved my sense of self-worth considerably.

• How can unrealistic expectations of "quick change" in our lives prove to be a major hindrance to our progress?

• Do you really think that you can view yourself any differently than you always have? If not, why?

Lord, I need You to . . .

DAY 52 _____

CHANGE IS A PROCESS

"The kingdom of God is like a man who casts seed upon
the soil; and goes to bed at night and gets up by day, and
the seed sprouts up and grows—how, he himself does not
know. The soil produces crops by itself; first the blade, then
the head. But when the crop permits, he immediately puts
in the sickle, because the harvest has come."
MARK 4:26–29

MANY OF MY PAST MEMORIES ARE STILL PAINFUL FOR ME, AND I
imagine they always will be. But through Christ, my
present attitude about myself is continually changing.
Knowing that I have no reason to feel ashamed has
motivated me to pursue a number of challenges that I
wouldn't have even considered pursuing a number of
years ago. In the process, I have experienced failure and
success. God has used each instance to teach me that
despite my circumstances, my worth is secure in Him.

We need to be honest about the pain, the anger, the
disappointment, and the loneliness of our past. We need
to put ourselves in relationships that will encourage us to
feel what we may have suppressed for many years. This
will enable us to begin (or continue) to experience hope,
and eventually, healing. Change is possible, but it is a
process.

Does this seem strange? Does it seem difficult? We may have difficulty relinquishing what is familiar (though painful) for what is unfamiliar because our fear of the unknown often seems stronger than the pain of a poor self-concept. It seems right to hang on. Proverbs 16:25 says, *There is a way which seems right to a man, but its end is the way of death.*

Any change in our behavior requires a release from our old self-concept, which is often founded in failure and the expectations of others. We need to learn how to relate to ourselves in a new way. To accomplish this, we must begin to base our self-worth on God's opinion of us and trust in His Spirit to accomplish change in our lives. Then, and only then, can we overcome Satan's deception that strongly influences our self-perception and behavior.

———————

• In what ways are you afraid of change in your life?

• Why would we tend to cling to the "painful familiar" instead of reaching, learning, and growing?

God, as I struggle to make the right choices, to grow, and heal, I am grateful to You for . . .

128

DAY 53 _____

PUT ON THE NEW SELF

That, in reference to your former manner of life, you lay
aside the old self, which is being corrupted in accordance
with the lusts of deceit, and that you be renewed in the
spirit of your mind, and put on the new self, which in the
likeness of God has been created in righteousness and
holiness of the truth.

EPHESIANS 4:22–24

WHEN WE TRUST CHRIST AND EXPERIENCE NEW LIFE,
forgiveness, and love, our lives will begin to change. Still,
regeneration does not affect an instantaneous change in
the full realm of our performance. We will continue to
stumble and fall at times, but the Scriptures clearly
instruct us to choose to act in ways that reflect our new
lives and values in Christ.

We are to *put on*, or envelop ourselves in, this new
self that progressively expresses Christian character in
our attitudes and behavior. We are marvelously unique,
created to reflect the character of Christ through our
individual personalities and behavior. Each believer, in a
different and special way, has the capability to shine
forth the light of God. No two will reflect His light in
exactly the same way.

The truth of regeneration can dispel the specter of
the past. Our sins have been forgiven, and we now have

129

tremendous capabilities for growth and change because we are new people with the Spirit of God living in us. Yes, when we sin, we will experience its destructive effects and the Father's discipline, but our sin will never change the truth of who we are in Christ.

- Describe how to "put on the new self."

- Read Ephesians 4:22–24. What process do you need to go through in order to experience your new self?

Father, thank You for . . .

DAY 54 _____

IT IS FINISHED!

"And others are the ones on whom seed was sown among the thorns; these are the ones who have heard the word, and the worries of the world, and the deceitfulness of riches, and the desires for other things enter in and choke the word, and it becomes unfruitful. And those are the ones on whom seed was sown on the good soil; and they hear the word and accept it, and bear fruit, thirty, sixty, and a hundredfold."

MARK 4:18–20

OUR REDEMPTION WAS MADE COMPLETE AT CALVARY. WHEN Jesus lifted up His eyes and cried, *It is finished!* (John 19:30), He told us that the provision for man's reconciliation with God was complete. Nothing more need be done, because the Word of life had been spoken to all mankind. Man needed only to hear the Word, accept it, and place his hope and trust in Christ.

But if the redemption we enjoy is complete, why do we so often fail to see the changes in our lives we long for? Why do we wrestle day after day with the same temptations, the same failings, and the same distractions we have always fought? Why can't we break free and move on toward maturity?

Christ illustrated the reasons for our lack of fruitfulness in the parable of the sower in Mark 4:3–20.

131

In agriculture, productivity depends on the fertility of the soil, the climate, and the presence or absence of weeds. The reasons Christ gave for lack of fruit in the believer's life were: Satan's taking away the Word of God, persecution, and the worries of the world. For most of us, the worries of the world are the primary culprit for our lack of growth.

In the context of honesty, affirmation, and patience, we can focus on the forgiveness we have received, and reject the deception and worldly desires that choke out the Word of life. We need to base our lives on God's Word and allow His character to be reproduced within us by the power of His Spirit.

———————

• What are some factors which are encouraging your spiritual growth?

• What factors are hindering your growth?

Dear Lord, as I identify the areas of my life that are preventing progress in my growth, I confess . . .

Day 55 _____

OUR SOURCE OF CHANGE

And I will ask the Father, and He will give you another
Helper, that He may be with you forever.
                    JOHN 14:16

THE TRUTHS WE HAVE EXAMINED IN THIS BOOK CAN HAVE
tremendous implications on our every goal and
relationship, but now we need to understand how to
actually implement them in our lives. How can we begin
to experience positive change? Jesus answered this
question in His last time of intimate instruction with His
disciples (John 13–16). He told them that He would soon
be put to death, but that they would not be left alone.
That Helper is the Holy Spirit. The Holy Spirit, the third
Person of the Trinity, is God and possesses all the
attributes of deity. His primary purpose is to glorify Christ
and bring attention to Him. Christ said, *He shall glorify
Me; for He shall take of Mine, and shall disclose it to you*
(John 16:14). The Holy Spirit is our teacher, and He
guides us into the truth of the Scriptures (John 16:13). It
is by His power that the love of Christ flows through us
and produces spiritual fruit within us (John 7:37–39;
15:1–8). This spiritual fruit is described in many ways in
the New Testament, including: intimate friendship with
Christ (John 15:14); love for one another (John 15:12); joy

and peace in the midst of difficulties (John 14:27; 15:11); steadfastness (Ephesians 5:18–21); and evangelism and discipleship (Matthew 28:18–20).

––––––––––

• Describe the blend and balance of the *Holy Spirit's* responsibility and *your* responsibility for your growth.

Thank You for the guidance and peace I have from Your Holy Spirit . . .

JOURNAL_____WEEK 11

From my reflection this week, I learned . . .

   . . . about God.

   . . . about myself.

   . . . about my motivations.

One thing I want to apply is:

Lord, I hope . . .

Lord, I need you to . . .

Day 56 _____

BEARING FRUIT

I am the true vine, and My Father is the vine dresser.
Abide in (live, grow, and gain your sustenance from) Me,
and I in you. As the branch cannot bear fruit of itself, unless
it abides in the vine, so neither can you, unless you abide in
Me. I am the vine, you are the branches; he who abides in
Me, and I in him, he bears much fruit; for apart from Me you
can do nothing.

JOHN 15:1, 4–5

OBVIOUSLY, THIS FRUIT IS NOT ALWAYS EVIDENT IN THE LIVES OF
Christians, but why not? As we all know, the Christian
life is not an easy one. It is not simply a self-improvement
program. True, we may at times be able to make some
changes in our habits through our own discipline and
determination, but Christianity is not merely self-effort.
The Christian life is a supernatural one in which we draw
on Christ as our resource for direction, encouragement,
and strength. In one of the most widely-known metaphors
of the Bible, Christ described the Christian life in John
15, using the illustration of a branch and a vine.

In terms of that which honors Christ, is spiritually
nourishing to us, and is genuine Christian service,
anything done apart from the love and power of Christ
amounts to nothing. Although we may expend tremendous
effort at a great personal cost, only that which is done for

Christ's glory in the power of His Spirit is of eternal value.

• Describe how a branch produces fruit (John 15:4–5).

• What are some evidences of spiritual fruit within the believer's life?

I am Your child. As a part of You, I desire to . . .

DAY 57_____

THE FRUIT OF THE SPIRIT

But the fruit of the Spirit is love, joy, peace, patience, kindness, goodness, faithfulness, gentleness, self-control . . .

GALATIANS 5:22–23

As WE RESPOND TO THE LOVE OF CHRIST AND TRUST HIS SPIRIT to fill us, these characteristics will become increasingly evident in our lives. The filling of the Holy Spirit includes two major aspects: our purpose (to bring honor to Christ instead of to ourselves) and our resources (trusting in His love and power to accomplish results, instead of trusting in our own wisdom and abilities). Although we will continue to mature in our relationship with the Lord over the years, we can begin to experience His love, strength, and purpose from the moment we put Him at the center of our lives.

Are you depending on God's Spirit to teach you, change you, and use you in the lives of others? If so, continue trusting Him! If not, identify any obstructions in your relationship with Him. Are there specific sins you need to confess?

Confession means to agree with God that you have sinned and that Christ has completely forgiven you. It also means "to repent," to turn from your sins to a life of love and obedience to God.

139

As you continue in the process of experiencing more of God's grace, take time to reflect on His love and power. Trust Him to guide you by His Word, fill you with His Spirit, and enable you to live for Him and be used by Him in the lives of others. Abiding in Christ does not mean deliverance from all of your problems, but it will provide a powerful relationship with the One who is the source of wisdom for difficult decisions, love to encourage you, and strength to help you endure.

———————

• Why do you need a Helper?

Father, I trust You to teach me, change me, and use me for Your purposes. Thank You for . . .

DAY 58 _____

REPLACING FALSE BELIEFS

Teach my Thy way, O Lord,
    And lead me in a level path,
    Because of my foes.
Do not deliver me over to the desire of my adversaries;
    For false witnesses have risen against me,
    And such as breathe out violence,
I would have despaired unless I had believed that
    I would see the goodness of the Lord
    In the land of the living.
Wait for the Lord;
    Be strong, and let your heart take courage;
    Yes, wait for the Lord.

                     PSALM 27:11–14

FOR MANY OF US, THE MAJORITY OF OUR BELIEFS WERE FORMED before we became Christians; therefore, it is easy to understand why many of our actions do not reflect Christ's character. Until those false beliefs are identified, ruthlessly rooted out, and replaced with biblical convictions, our lives will continue to be filled with destructive thoughts and actions.

Because of our fallen human nature, all of us experience false beliefs which contradict God's Word. Failure to recognize them can have devastating effects on our lives.

For example, a young girl named Dawn was sent to me by her parents, who hoped I could reason with her about her promiscuous behavior. But Dawn could not understand how something that felt so good and made her so happy could be wrong.

Over the course of several weeks, Dawn began to discuss her circumstances more openly with me. She explained that her father spent so much time working that he had little time for her and her mother. Dawn had been neglected, and after several meetings together, her wall of defenses eroded and she cried, "I just want to be loved, that's all!" Her behavior had been her unconscious attempt to feel close to someone. She had enjoyed it primarily because she finally felt loved, even though most of these men were really using her and not loving her at all.

Dawn eventually joined a support group, where she met other young women who were learning about the pain of their past and their hope for the future. These women could identify with Dawn's dreams and fears. They encouraged her and each other to gain a new sense of identity based on their love for each other and the truth of God's Word. This process hasn't been easy for Dawn, but her progress is real.

———————

• How can people affect your ability to replace false beliefs with God's truth?

*I'm grateful, dear Lord, for the good role-models
You have placed in my life, and I want to be a good
example for others, as well . . .*

DAY 59 _____

REJECT/REPLACE

Finally, brethren, whatever is true, whatever is
honorable, whatever is right, whatever is pure, whatever is
lovely, whatever is of good repute, if there is any excellence
and if anything worthy of praise, let your mind dwell on
these things. The things you have learned and received
and heard and seen in me, practice these things; and the
God of peace shall be with you.

PHILIPPIANS 4:8–9

ONE OF THE GREATEST CHARACTERISTICS OF PERSONAL MATURITY
in Christ is the ability to be honest about how we really
feel about a person or situation, and the willingness to
accept full responsibility for our emotional and behavioral
reactions in the disturbing circumstances of life. In
realizing that our circumstances aren't the cause of our
self-destructive reactions, and by applying God's truths
to those situations, we can gain peace and perspective.

The world need not have control over us. Our spiritual
battles may be intense, but we will be able to persevere if
we can begin to analyze our circumstances through God's
perspective and reject the false beliefs which often control
our emotions and actions. Faith in God's Word prevents
us from being buffeted by difficult situations, or having to
live "under the circumstances."

Identifying our false beliefs is the first step on our path toward new freedom in Jesus Christ. Once we recognize that many of our deeply-held beliefs are actually rooted in deception, we can begin using our emotions as a checkpoint to determine if we are basing our beliefs about a given circumstance on the truth or lies. Many of our painful emotions, such as fear, anger, and tension, are often the product of believing Satan's lies. Therefore, when we experience these emotions, we can ask ourselves, *What am I believing in this situation?* In almost every case, we will be able to trace our negative emotions back to one of Satan's false beliefs. We can then choose to reject the lie we have identified and replace it with the corresponding truth from the Scriptures. This process is amazingly simple, yet profound and applicable.

———————

• What are some true and honorable things you can choose to dwell on?

• How will focusing on these things affect you?

Lord, please help me to . . .

DAY 60 _____

RESPONDING TO EMOTIONS

Trust in Him at all times, O people;
  Pour out your heart before Him;
  God is a refuge for us.
                    PSALM 62:8

IN EXAMINING OUR EMOTIONS, IT IS IMPORTANT TO REALIZE THAT not all distressing emotions reflect deception. For example, the emotion of remorse might be the Holy Spirit's conviction leading us to repentance. Anger with someone for molesting a child or beating an elderly person is righteous anger, just as a measure of fear while driving during rush hour is entirely justifiable!

In our problem-filled world, there are at least two ways that many of us choose to deal with our emotions and surrounding circumstances. One is to shut them out completely, refusing to acknowledge their presence or to be affected by them; the other is to become enslaved to them.

Switching off our emotions can cause us to become callous and insensitive to ourselves and those around us. Unfortunately, this is just what happened to Mike.

Over the years, Mike had deadened himself to his emotions, apparently not allowing anything to bother him. He had experienced a difficult childhood, first being abandoned by his parents, and then being shuffled from one relative to another. In an effort to stop the pain, Mike learned to block out his feelings and to ignore his circumstances.

Melinda, on the other hand, wore her emotions on her sleeve. She wasn't difficult to figure out. Her flaring temper, her torrent of tears, and her jovial laughter were all indications of her rollercoaster emotions. Never knowing what to expect, Melinda's husband, Ken, became weary of trying to deal with his volatile wife.

Melinda's erratic mood swings affected her so much that they became, in effect, her lord. Her feelings seemed to be more real than anything else in her life and they clouded her perception of God and His purposes.

• In what ways do you express your emotions?

• In what ways are you enslaved to them?

Dealing with my emotions—allowing myself to feel them and responding to them in a healthy way—requires a lot of thought, effort, and guidance from You. Father, I trust You to . . .

JOURNAL _____ WEEK 12

From my reflection this week, I learned . . .

. . . about God.

. . . about myself.

. . . about my motivations.

One thing I want to apply is:

Lord, I hope . . .

Lord, I need you to . . .

DAY 61_____

EMOTIONS, A GIFT FROM GOD

My heart is in anguish within me,
   And the terrors of death have fallen upon me.
Fear and trembling come upon me;
   And horror has overwhelmed me.

PSALM 55:4–5

WE OFTEN RESPOND INCORRECTLY TO THEM, BUT OUR EMOTIONS are in fact a gift from God, intended to be used and enjoyed. Emotions are signals which tell us something about our environment. They can protect us by helping us to choose appropriate behavior. We can help ourselves (and others) by encouraging honesty and by allowing ourselves to fully experience both our positive and negative feelings. Emotions help us to determine what is really going on inside. In the same way that good parents allow their children to express hurt, and experience comfort and healing when they have fallen, we can do this for ourselves and others by advocating an honest expression of emotions and by applying comfort to the hurts each of us experience. In this way, we can avoid repression and denial, and encourage an appropriate expression of our emotions—within ourselves, with others, and with God.

The inability to experience and express feelings is as dangerous to our well-being as the inability to feel physical pain. As we become aware of painful emotions and destructive behavior, we need to acknowledge these feelings and actions to God in prayer, asking Him to reveal any false beliefs that may be hindering our fellowship with Him. Then, empowered by the Holy Spirit, and encouraged by the love and affirmation of others, we can learn to cast aside our false beliefs and choose to believe the truths of God's Word.

It is necessary to first expose our root emotions and the false beliefs which are triggering them. Then, by faith, we can allow God's Word to renew our minds.

———————

• Why are your emotions a gift from God?

Thank You, dear God, for . . .

DAY 62 _____

FAMILY FORTRESSES

For though we walk in the flesh, we do not war according
to the flesh, for the weapons of our warfare are not of the
flesh, but divinely powerful for the destruction of fortresses.
We are destroying speculations and every lofty thing raised
up against the knowledge of God, and we are taking every
thought captive to the obedience of Christ.

2 CORINTHIANS 10:3–5

FOR MANY OF US, OUR FAMILY BACKGROUNDS HAVE BEEN VERY
painful. Alcoholism, drug abuse, divorce, workaholism,
violence, or other family disorders have left us with deep
emotional scars. We may feel neglected, lonely, angry,
hurt, or numb. We may consequently believe that we are
unlovable people who are unworthy of being cared for by
others, and that God is like our parents: harsh,
condemning, manipulative, or aloof. These emotions and
self-perceptions form a strong fortress that has been
founded on Satan's lies and communicated to us by those
who were supposed to love, protect, and provide for us.
Concepts like these don't vanish quickly. Often, our first
step toward progress is realizing that we have been hurting
for a long time, but have refused to admit it, or perhaps,
that our defense mechanisms of drivenness or withdrawal
have been protecting us from the reality of our pain.

Through the process of being honest and experiencing

comfort from the Lord and others, these fortresses can be slowly torn down. They are overcome by *destroying speculations and every lofty thing raised up against the knowledge of God;* that is, by identifying and rejecting specific lies, and then replacing them with the truth.

• How has your family contributed to the fortress of painful, repressed emotions and faulty perceptions?

• How can this fortress be torn down?

Heavenly Father, please open my eyes, and help me to identify the issues in my life that need to be dealt with. I desire to . . .

DAY 63_____

TRUE REPENTANCE

I now rejoice, not that you were made sorrowful, but that you were made sorrowful to the point of repentance; for you were made sorrowful according to the will of God, in order that you might not suffer loss in anything through us. For the sorrow that is according to the will of God produces a repentance without regret, leading to salvation; but the sorrow of the world produces death.

2 CORINTHIANS 7:9–10

THE CORINTHIANS' EXAMPLE DEMONSTRATES REPENTANCE AS A tactical weapon of our spiritual warfare. *Repentance* means "to change"; to change one's mind, purpose, and actions. It is more than just the experience of sorrow; it is the changing of our attitude and actions when we have realized that they are sinful and dishonoring to God.

As an offensive weapon, repentance has two sharp edges. The first allows us to discern and reject false beliefs.

The second edge of repentance is the replacement of false beliefs with the truth of God's Word. By affirming God's truth about our worth, we will lodge it deep within our hearts and minds, and begin to reshape our thinking, feelings, and behavior. Then, the process of having the truth modeled to us, affirmed in us, taught to us, and applied by us over time will enable us to increasingly experience freedom in different areas of our lives.

153

If false beliefs remain in our minds, unchallenged and unrejected, they retain an unconscious influence on our emotions and reactions. Consequently, our warfare is a sustained and continuous battle. Every disturbing situation provides us with an opportunity to discover our incorrect thinking, to reject our world-acquired beliefs, and exchange them for the truth. This is a daily process for every Christian; only this aggressive, conscious, truth-seeking effort can reverse years of habitually wrong thinking.

———————

- What is genuine repentance?

Thank You for the spiritual weapon of repentance. As I struggle to turn away from sin, I praise You, dear Lord, for Your endless mercy and grace . . .

DAY 64_____

RIVETED ON GOD'S WORD

But I say, walk by the Spirit, and you will not carry out
the desire of the flesh. For the flesh sets its desire against
the Spirit, and the Spirit against the flesh; for these are in
opposition to one another, so that you may not do the
things that you please.

GALATIANS 5:16–17

*AFFIRMING THE TRUTHS OF THE SCRIPTURES DOES NOT MEAN
that our natural mind will agree with what we are
affirming.* The Bible teaches that the natural mind is
antagonistic toward God. It may be uncomfortable to
reflect on the truths of God's Word because they oppose
the lies of the enemy. Don't be surprised by spiritual
conflict when you confront these lies with God's truths.

*Realize that we can't hope to achieve spiritual growth
and change through self-effort.* The Holy Spirit is our
Helper, and He will point out those circumstances in
which we are believing Satan's lies; He will give us insight
into the truth of the Scriptures; and He will give us
strength to persevere in spiritual battle. Even our desire
to honor Christ is due to the Holy Spirit's work in our
lives. Through His wisdom and power, and through our
moment-by-moment choice to follow Him, the Holy Spirit
produces changes in our lives for the glory of Christ.

In order to become proficient at affirming these truths,

155

we need to become students of God's Word, and allow its truth to lodge deep within our hearts and minds. We should make it a regular practice to meditate upon the Scriptures so that the Holy Spirit can use them to change our beliefs, thoughts, emotions, and actions.

Learn to confront each false belief with a specific truth from God's Word. Once we have identified a specific false belief, we should claim God's corresponding truth in the situation.

• How can you learn to perceive the enemy's schemes more clearly?

• How can God's truth help you in spiritual conflict?

Father, when I am confronted by one of Satan's lies, please give me the wisdom and discernment I need to battle his deception with Your truths. Please show me . . .

DAY 65 _____

NO CONDEMNATION!

There is therefore now no condemnation for those who
are in Christ Jesus.

ROMANS 8:1

WHEN I SHARED THIS IMPORTANT TRUTH WITH A TROUBLED
Christian brother, his jaw dropped and his eyes filled
with tears. He looked at me incredulously and exclaimed,
"You mean, all this guilt I have been carrying for so long
is unnecessary? I can be free from these tormenting
feelings of condemnation? Why hasn't somebody told me
this before?"

The Apostle Paul has been trying to tell us just that
for centuries, but few of us have listened. We feel we
deserve condemnation, and we fail to realize that Christ
has freed us from the guilt and condemnation our sins
deserve.

Perhaps no emotion is more destructive than guilt. It
causes a loss of self-respect. It causes the human spirit to
wither, and eats away at our personal significance. Guilt
is a strong motivator, but it plays on our fears of failure
and rejection; therefore, it can never ultimately build,
encourage, or inspire us in our desire to live for Christ.

_____

- How has guilt affected you?

Christ, You have taken away my sins. You have freed me from guilt and condemnation. I feel overwhelmed by the magnitude of Your love and forgiveness for me . . .

JOURNAL _____ WEEK 13

From my reflection this week, I learned . . .

   . . . about God.

   . . . about myself.

   . . . about my motivations.

One thing I want to apply is:

Lord, I hope . . .

Lord, I need you to . . .

DAY 66 _____

GUILT AND CONSEQUENCES

For all have sinned and fall short of the glory of God,
being justified as a gift by His grace through the redemption
which is in Christ Jesus.

ROMANS 3:23–24

SOME OF US UNDERSTAND GUILT AS A SENSE OF LEGAL AND moral accountability before God. We may try to distinguish it from low self-esteem by reasoning that guilt is the result of a sinful act or moral wrongdoing, while low self-esteem is derived from a feeling of social or personal inadequacy. Consequently, a lie makes us feel unacceptable to God and brings guilt, while bad table manners make us feel unacceptable to the people around us and bring low self-esteem.

This perspective shows some depth of thought, but it focuses on an emotional response to guilt rather than its root cause. At its root, guilt is the condition of being separated from God and of deserving condemnation for sin. Low self-esteem can be experienced by Christians or non-Christians—anyone who believes Satan's lies and feels like a failure, hopeless and rejected.

As we have determined, guilt has a restricted meaning in the New Testament. It refers only to man's condition prior to his salvation. Only the non-Christian is actually guilty before God. He has transgressed the law of God

161

and must face the consequences. Guilt shakes its fist and says, "You have fallen short and must pay the price. You are personally accountable." Our condemnation is removed only through Christ. He took all of our guilt upon Himself when He accepted the penalty for our sins and suffered the full punishment for all sin. Because of His substitution, we need never face guilt's consequences. We are acquitted and absolved from guilt, free from our sentence of spiritual death.

- How does Christ's death on the cross deal with our guilt?

When I think about the price You paid for my sins, Heavenly Father, I feel . . .

DAY 67 _____

OVERCOMING GUILT

Who gave Himself for us, that He might redeem us from
every lawless deed and purify for Himself a people for His
own possession, zealous for good deeds.
TITUS 2:14

MANY OF US HAVE BEEN TOLD THAT WE ARE STILL GUILTY EVEN
after we have trusted Christ to pay for our sins. And
sadly, we have heard this in churches—places that should
be loudly and clearly proclaiming the forgiveness and
freedom found in the cross. Perhaps some people think
that if they don't use guilt motivation, we won't do
anything. Guilt may motivate us for a short while, until
we adjust to being properly motivated. But a short period
of waiting is well worth the long-term results of grace-
oriented, intrinsic motivation.

Learn to identify incorrect teaching, guilt motivation,
and the results of guilt in your own thoughts. Then,
refuse to believe the lies any longer, and focus instead on
the unconditional love and forgiveness of Christ. His love
is powerful, and He is worthy of our intense zeal to obey
and honor Him. The result of proper motivation is an
enduring, deepening commitment to Christ and His cause,
rather than the prevalent results of guilt motivation:
resentment and the desire to escape.

_____

- Think of the last time you were motivated by guilt to do something. If you had reremembered God's truth about you—that you are deeply loved, completely forgiven, fully pleasing, totally accepted, and absolutely complete in Christ—how do you think your emotions and actions would have been different?

Dear Lord, as I continue to focus on You and Your truth, please help me to . . .

DAY 68_____

GUILT AND CONVICTION

"And He, when He comes, will convict the world
concerning sin, and righteousness, and judgment."
JOHN 16:8

CHRISTIANS ARE FREED FROM GUILT, BUT WE ARE STILL SUBJECT
to conviction. The Bible frequently speaks of the Holy
Spirit's work to convict believers of sin. He directs and
encourages our spiritual progress by revealing our sins in
contrast to the holiness and purity of Christ.

Although the Holy Spirit convicts both believers and
unbelievers of sin (John 16:8), His conviction of believers
is not intended to produce pangs of guilt. Our status and
self-worth are secure by the grace of God, and we are no
longer guilty. Conviction deals with our behavior, not our
status before God. Conviction is the Holy Spirit's way of
showing the error of our performance in light of God's
standard and truth. His motivation is love, correction,
and protection.

While guilt is applicable to non-believers, and
originates from Satan, conviction is the privilege of those
who believe, and is given by the Holy Spirit. Guilt brings
depression and despair, but conviction enables us to realize
the beauty of God's forgiveness and to experience His love
and power.

———————

- **What are some differences between guilt and conviction?**

I am thankful for the Holy Spirit's loving conviction and guidance . . .

DAY 69 _____

RESPONDING TO FEELINGS OF GUILT

And He died for all, that they who live should no longer live for themselves, but for Him who died and rose again on their behalf.

2 CORINTHIANS 5:15

How CAN WE DEAL WITH FEELINGS OF GUILT? FIRST, WE NEED to affirm that Christ has forgiven us and has made us judicially righteous before God. Our sin does not result in condemnation, but it is harmful and brings dishonor to God. We can confess our sin to God, claim the forgiveness we already have in Christ, and then move on in joy and freedom to honor Him. The following prayer expresses this attitude:

Father, I affirm that I am deeply loved by You, that I am fully pleasing to You, and that I am totally accepted in Your sight. You have made me complete and have given me the righteousness of Christ, even though my performance often falls short. Lord, I confess my sins to You. (List them. Be specific.) I agree with You that these are wrong. Thank You for Your grace and forgiveness. Is there anything I need to return, anyone I need to repay, or anyone I need to apologize to? Thank You.

It is important to affirm our righteousness in Christ as well as to confess our sins. God does not need to be reminded of our right standing in Him, but we do. Therefore, we need to make this prayer a daily experience and allow it to pervade our thoughts and hearts. As we yield to the gentle prodding of God-given conviction, confess our sins, and affirm our true relationship with Him, we will be gradually shaped and molded in such a way that we will increasingly honor the One who *died and rose again on [our] behalf* (2 Corinthians 5:15).

We may not experience joy and freedom immediately, especially if we have developed the painful habit of prolonged self-condemnation as a way of dealing with sin. Loving friends who listen to us and encourage us can be an example of God's forgiveness to us. As we become more honest about our feelings through these affirming relationships, we will be able to increasingly experience the freedom, forgiveness, and freshness of God's grace.

- How do unrealistic expectations about our feelings keep us from experiencing God's love and forgiveness?

Thank You, Lord, for Your unconditional love and forgiveness. Daily, I am becoming more aware of how complete I am in You. Please help me to continue growing in Your Spirit by showing me . . .

168

DAY 70_____

CHRIST: BEDROCK OF OUR FAITH

So faith comes by hearing, and hearing by the word of
Christ.

ROMANS 10:17

WE HAVE SEEN THAT OUR RELATIONSHIP WITH GOD, OUR
security, and our self-worth are not earned by our efforts.
They are obtained only by faith. This point is so important,
let's take some time to analyze what faith is.

Faith has several synonyms: *trust, dependence,
reliance,* and *belief.* The focus is on the object of faith, not
the faith itself. For example, if I believe that a certain
chair will hold me when I sit in it, the primary issue is the
construction and quality of the chair—the *object* of my
faith, not the *amount* of faith I have. Even if I believe very
strongly that the chair will support me, if the chair is a
rotten, broken-down piece of junk, then it will break if I
try to sit in it. My faith will not make it a good chair. But
if the chair is of quality construction, it takes very little
faith to sit comfortably in it. Again, it is the quality of the
object, not the quantity of my faith, that is of primary
importance.

In Christianity, Christ is the object of faith, and faith
is our trust in His character and abilities. The more we
know Him, the more we will trust Him. Faith, then,
requires our knowing God, and knowing Him requires a

169

relationship. To know God, we need to talk to Him through prayer, listen to His voice, see Him at work in our lives and the lives of others, and search out His will and deeds through the Scriptures He has given us.

• What are some differences between trusting in Christ and trusting in feelings? . . . or trusting in people's opinions of you? . . . or your performance?

*I get my security and self-worth from my faith in Christ. The issue is the **object** of my faith, not the **amount** of my faith.*

When I reflect on Your unconditional love for me, Your forgiveness of me, Your constant concern for me . . . I realize I have everything I need for a healthy sense of self-worth and security . . .

JOURNAL _____ WEEK 14

From my reflection this week, I learned . . .

    . . . about God.

    . . . about myself.

    . . . about my motivations.

One thing I want to apply is:

Lord, I hope . . .

Lord, I need you to . . .

Day 71_____

COMPLETE IN HIM

For in Him (Christ) all the fullness of Deity dwells in
    bodily form,
  and in Him you have been made complete,
  and He is the head over all rule and authority.
                        COLOSSIANS 2:9–10

THROUGH THE GIFT OF GOD'S GRACE, WE ARE SPIRITUALLY alive, forgiven, and complete in Him. In the church at Colossae, false teachers taught that "completeness" came through a combination of philosophy, good works, other religions, and Christ. Paul's clear message was that we are made complete through Christ alone. To attempt to find completeness through any other source, including success, the approval of others, prestige, or appearance, is to be taken captive through philosophy and empty deception (Colossians 2:8). Nothing can add to the death of Christ to pay for our sins and the resurrection of Christ to give us new life. We are complete because Christ has forgiven us and given us life—the capacity for growth and change.

According to the theologian, Louis Berkhof, "Regeneration consists in the implanting of the principle of the new spiritual life in man, in a radical change of the governing disposition of the soul, which, under the influence of the Holy Spirit, gives birth to a life that moves in a Godward direction. In principle this change affects the whole man: the intellect . . . the will . . . and the feelings or emotions."*

————————

• Do you believe you have the capacity for growth and change? Why or why not?

Father, I am excited about growing and changing. The desire of my heart is to know all that You would have me to learn about myself and relating to others in a way that is honoring to You . . .

*Louis Berkhof, *Systematic Theology* (Grand Rapids, MI: William B. Eerdmans Publishing Company, 1941), p. 468.

DAY 72 _____

RESPONDING TO IMPURE MOTIVES

... we have as our ambition ... to be pleasing to Him.
2 CORINTHIANS 5:9

As YOU RECOGNIZE CORRECT MOTIVES FOR OBEDIENCE, AND AS you are able to identify improper motivations in your life, you may think, *I've never done anything purely for the Lord in my whole life!* You may feel a sense of pain and remorse for your inappropriate motives. But don't sink into a state of morbid introspection, demeaning yourself for your past attitudes. There are at least two perspectives that will help you focus on the Lord and grow in a godly desire to honor Him.

First, obedience from a right motivation is a choice. It is not based on how you feel. At any and every point in your life (like right now) you can actively, consciously choose to honor Christ. The Lord wants you to live by your godly choices, not by your fickle emotions. Ask the Holy Spirit to help you develop a sense of intensity about this choice.

Second, since your motives are usually a reflection of what you believe, they will begin to change as your belief system changes. Consistently considering and applying God's truth will have a profound and far-reaching impact on your motives. As you reject Satan's lies, you will gradually be *transformed by the renewing of your mind* ...

(Romans 12:2), and will have an increasing desire to honor the One who loves you and purchased you by His own blood.

So, as an act of your will, choose to honor the Lord no matter what your emotions tell you, and consistently learn and apply the truths of God's Word so that they will begin to pervade your thoughts. Your motives won't become totally pure until you see the Lord face to face (1 John 3:2), but the better you know Him, the more you will see that He is worthy of your love, loyalty, and obedience.

• Have you felt that your motives had to be completely pure for you to be honoring to God?

• Why is this unrealistic?

Thank You, Father, for Your patience while I grow in my desire to honor You . . .

DAY 73 _____

REALIZING OUR RECONCILIATION

And although you were formerly alienated and hostile in
mind, engaged in evil deeds, yet He has now reconciled
you in His fleshly body through death, in order to present
you before Him holy and blameless and beyond reproach.
COLOSSIANS 1:21–22

IS THERE ANYTHING A CHRISTIAN CAN DO TO BECOME MORE
acceptable to God? No! If there were, then the cross would
be insufficient. If we can do anything to be more acceptable
to God, then Christ either lied or was mistaken when He
cried out on the cross, *"It is finished!"* (John 19:30). If that
is the case, what He should have said was, "It is almost
finished, and if you live a perfect life, you and I together
might make you acceptable."

Since our relationship with God was bought entirely
by the blood of Christ, it is the height of pride to think
that our own good works can make us acceptable to God.
The Bible speaks to the contrary: *He saved us, not on the
basis of deeds which we have done in righteousness, but
according to His mercy* ... (Titus 3:5). Christ has reconciled
us to God and He allows us to experience the incredible
truth, *We are totally accepted by and acceptable to God.*

What should we do when we have failed or when
someone disapproves of us? A practical way of
summarizing the truth we've examined is:

177

It would be nice if_____(my
boss liked me, I could fix the refrigerator, my complexion
were clear, James had picked me up on time, or . . .), but
I'm still deeply loved, completely forgiven, fully pleasing,
totally accepted, and complete in Christ.

This statement doesn't mean that we won't feel pain or anger. We need to be honest about our feelings. A statement like the one above is simply a way to quickly gain God's perspective on whatever we are experiencing. It is not magic, but it enables us to reflect on the implications of biblical truth. We can apply this truth in every difficult situation, whether it is someone's disapproval, our own failure to accomplish something, or the failure of another person.

Memorize the truth in the above statement and begin to apply it in your situations and relationships.

———————

- How will utilizing this statement affect your thoughts, emotions, and behavior?

Jesus, I ask You for clarity of thought today as I apply the above statement to my everyday situations and relationships . . .

DAY 74_____

RESPONDING TO OUR CHILDREN

Fathers, do not provoke your children to anger; but bring
them up in the discipline and instruction of the Lord.

EPHESIANS 6:4

W HEN THEIR CHILDREN GET INTO TROUBLE, PARENTS USUALLY
alternate between blaming themselves and blaming their
children. After all, someone has to be blamed. The problem
in either case is not that parents are loving their child too
much or too little, but that their personal significance is
wrapped up in their performance as parents. Therefore,
when the child does well, the parents feel good about
themselves. When a child does poorly, however, they
often blame each other or the child. Beneath it all is the
internalized and unconscious belief: *Someone has to take
the blame.*

Our worth is totally secure in Christ, so our children's
success or failure, cuteness or whining doesn't affect our
value in the least. We need to see our children the way
our heavenly Father sees us: *deeply loved, completely
forgiven, fully pleasing, and totally accepted.* Then, when
they disobey, our discipline will be like the Father's
discipline of us: in love, not anger. If we approach our
children with an attitude of grief rather than anger when
they disobey, it will make a tremendous difference! What
a difference it will make if we go to our children with the

179

attitude and words, "It's sad that you disobeyed. It was harmful to you, and I love you so much that I don't want you to harm yourself. I will need to discipline you to help you remember not to do it again. Remember, the reason I am disciplining you is that I love you so much!" . . . instead of, "You've done it again, and I'll make sure you regret it! I wonder if you'll ever amount to anything!"

Responding to our children in grief instead of anger will have monumental implications on both them and us. Our children won't be afraid of us, our relationship with them won't be marred by anger, and they will be more likely to view God as a loving Father rather than as a tyrant. As parents, we will have a more accurate perception of God's love and gracious discipline, and we will be more in control of our emotions. We won't try to deny that we are getting angry at our children's misbehavior, letting our anger build and build until we explode. Instead, we will be able to express our displeasure more quickly and acceptably because it will be wholesome grief instead of unholy anger. These are powerful and welcome implications, indeed!

––––––––

- How can the principle of responding to children's misbehavior out of grief affect them, you, and your relationship with them?

Father, please show me . . .

DAY 75 _____

FAITH AND FEELINGS

For the flesh sets its desire against the Spirit, and the
Spirit against the flesh; for these are in opposition to one
another.

GALATIANS 5:17

WHEN WE DEPEND ON GOD, WILL WE FEEL HIS LOVE AND
strength? Maybe, maybe not. Our culture would make us
think that our feelings are the most important way of
determining if our actions are valid. But as Christians,
we have a much higher authority than our feelings. We
have the truth of God's Word, and we can choose, as an
act of our will, to obey Him. Our will is paramount, not
our feelings. The French philosopher Fenelon said, "The
essence of Christianity resides in the will." Our feelings
may reflect the love of Christ as we forgive others, share
our faith, give generously, and demonstrate other spiritual
characteristics in our lives. But on many occasions, our
emotions are inconsistent, unpredictable, and
diametrically opposed to God's Word. Often, we refuse to
obey Him because we don't *feel* like it. For example, we
may be afraid to share our faith because someone might
reject us, or we may continue to indulge in sin because we
don't *feel* like stopping. But what about the times when
we earnestly want to obey God, and our emotions say,

NO!? Here are some possible reasons our feelings may oppose the ways of God:

1) Our sinful nature may be prompting us to disobey God.
2) We may be experiencing spiritual conflict.
3) It may be that our negative emotions are simply the residual feelings of the fear of failure or the fear of rejection that we are in the process of overcoming by claiming God's truth.

When you choose to believe God's Word, your emotions may not follow immediately. Does that mean you aren't trusting God? No. Faith is often exercised in the context of struggle, in the midst of conflicting thoughts and emotions. A look at the people of God in the Scriptures shows that their faith was not in the absence of doubts and struggles, but in the *face* of doubts and struggles. The idea that faith is only found apart from conflicting thoughts and emotions is one of Satan's schemes to confuse and discourage you. When we trust in God, we will experience many obstacles to faith, but placing our trust in His Word—not our feelings—will see us through.

• What is the relationship between faith and feelings?

• How can unrealistic expectations of our emotions be harmful to us?

Lord, please give me wisdom in knowing when my feelings are obedient to Your Word . . .

JOURNAL _____ WEEK 15

From my reflection this week, I learned . . .

. . . about God.

. . . about myself.

. . . about my motivations.

One thing I want to apply is:

Lord, I hope . . .

Lord, I need you to . . .

D<small>AY</small> 76_____

RENEWING THE MIND

And do not be conformed to this world, but be
transformed by the renewing of your mind, that you may
prove what the will of God is, that which is good and
acceptable and perfect.

R<small>OMANS</small> 12:2

I<small>T IS INTERESTING THAT WHEN THE</small> H<small>OLY</small> S<small>PIRIT GAVE US A NEW</small>
spirit, He did not give us a totally renewed mind. Although
the Spirit of Christ lives within us and enables us to
evaluate our experiences, our minds tend to dwell on the
worldly thoughts of our old nature instead of on God's
truth. We are in conflict, torn between our new godly
motivation to glorify Christ and our old motivations of
lust and pride. Paul recognized this conflict.

How can we grow in Christ? How can we assist in the
process that will enable us to follow Him? To change our
behavior, we usually need to see others who are being
honest, and who are in the process of applying spiritual
truths to their lives. In this environment, and through
our personal study of God's Word, we can reject earthly
thoughts and replace them with those that are spiritual.
Solomon wrote, *As [a man] thinks within himself, so he is*
(Proverbs 23:7). Our thoughts usually affect the way we
feel, the way we perceive ourselves and others, and
ultimately, the way we act. The way we think can

determine whether we will live according to God's truth or the world's value system.

———————

• What ideas, relationships, fantasies, or desires does your mind dwell on?

• How have these thoughts affected your emotions, behavior, and relationships?

Lord, being honest about my behavior, relationships, and feelings can be painful sometimes. Thank You for the Holy Spirit's help and unwavering conviction as I walk through this long journey of spiritual, relational, and emotional growth . . .

DAY 77 _____

NEWNESS OF LIFE

Blessed is the man who trusts in the Lord, whose confidence is in Him.

JEREMIAH 17:7

THE MOMENT YOU TRUST CHRIST, MANY WONDERFUL THINGS happen to you:

- All your sins are forgiven: past, present, and future (Colossians 2:13–14).
- You become a child of God (John 1:12; Romans 8:15).
- You receive eternal life (John 5:24).
- You are delivered from Satan's domain and transferred into the kingdom of Christ (Colossians 1:13).
- Christ comes to dwell within you (Colossians 1:27; Revelation 3:20).
- You become a new creation (2 Corinthians 5:17).
- You are declared righteous by God (2 Corinthians 5:21).
- You enter into a love relationship with God (1 John 4:9–11).
- You are accepted by God (Colossians 1:19–22).

_____

- Think on the implications of these truths in your life. Then, thank God for His wonderful grace and experience *the love of Christ which surpasses knowledge* (Ephesians 3:19).

Thank You, dear God, for . . .

DAY 78_____

DETERMINING OUR WORTH

And you were dead in your trespasses and sins, in which
you formerly walked according to the course of this world,
according to the prince of the power of the air, of the spirit
that is now working in the sons of disobedience. Among
them we too all formerly lived in the lusts of our flesh,
indulging the desires of the flesh and of the mind, and were
by nature children of wrath, even as the rest. But God,
being rich in mercy, because of His great love with which
He loved us, even when we were dead in our
transgressions, made us alive together with Christ (by
grace you have been saved).

EPHESIANS 2:1–5

IN THE BEGINNING, GOD DECLARED THAT MAN WAS CREATED TO
reign with Him; however, man rejected God's truth and
chose instead to believe Satan's lie. Today, man continues
to reject God's truth and offer of salvation through Jesus
Christ. He chooses instead to trust in his success and the
opinions of others to give him a sense of self-worth, though
the Scriptures clearly teach that apart from Christ, man
is enslaved to sin and condemned to an eternity in hell.

Since the Fall, man has often failed to turn to God for
the truth about himself. Instead, he has looked to others
to meet his inescapable need for self-worth. *I am what
others say I am,* he has reasoned. *I will find my value in
their opinions of me.*

189

Isn't it amazing that we turn to others who have a perspective as limited and darkened as our own to discover our worth! Rather than relying on God's steady, uplifting reassurance of who we are, we depend on others who base our worth on our ability to meet their standards.

———————

• Your actions and emotions are usually indicative of your belief system. Why do you do what you do, say what you say, and go where you go? How much of what you do is to honor God, and how much is to please people?

Lord, I'm thankful for the reassurance and security I find in You . . .

DAY 79_____

REJECTING THE LIE

"Behold, I have given you authority to tread upon
serpents and scorpions, and over all the power of the
enemy, and nothing shall injure you."
LUKE 10:19

IN SPITE OF ADAM AND EVE'S SIN, GOD'S PLAN IS TO BRING MAN
back to the destiny for which he was originally created—
to bear His image. To accomplish this, God gives a new
nature to all who believe in Christ. This new nature is
able to reflect God's character and rule His creation. In
Luke 10:19, Jesus spoke of the authority of this new
nature.

Satan, however, continues to deceive people, including
many Christians, into believing that the basis of their
worth is their performance and their ability to please
others. The equation below reflects Satan's lie:

SELF-WORTH = PERFORMANCE + OTHERS' OPINIONS

_____

- Can we overcome Satan's deception and reject this
  basis of our self-worth? Can we trust God's complete
  acceptance of us as His sons and daughters, and allow

Him to free us from our dependency on success and the approval of others? Rejecting Satan's lie and accepting God's evaluation of us leads to a renewed hope, joy, and purpose in life.

Father, thank You for Your total acceptance of me. I trust You to guide me out of the web of Satan's lies, and lead me away from . . .

DAY 80 _____

AFFIRMING RELATIONSHIPS

But we proved to be gentle among you, as a nursing
mother tenderly cares for her own children. Having thus a
fond affection for you, we were well-pleased to impart to
you not only the gospel of God but also our own lives,
because you had become very dear to us.

1 THESSALONIANS 2:7–8

PEOPLE SELDOM HAVE THE OBJECTIVITY AND THE COURAGE TO
be honest about reality in their lives without some
affirmation from others. The love, strength, and honesty
we find in other people are tangible expressions of those
traits that are characteristic of God. A friend, a small
group, a pastor, or a counselor who won't be frustrated by
our slow progress—and who won't give us quick and easy
solutions—is a valuable find! (Of course, it is always wise
to use discretion and discernment regarding what and
with whom we share. The act of sharing is a responsibility.)
Pray that God will provide a person or group of persons
with whom you can be open and honest, who can objectively
listen to you and share with you, and who will encourage
you to make real, rather than superficial progress.

———————

• Name someone who has affirmed and encouraged you
  in the past:

• How did this person's affirmation affect you?

• Who is affirming you now? What affect does this person
  have on you?

• Do you need to find someone who will encourage and
  affirm you? If so, how do you plan to find that person or
  group of people?

*I appreciate the affirmation and encouragement of
others. Father, today please show me ways I can be
affirming to them, too . . .*

JOURNAL _____ WEEK 16

From my reflection this week, I learned . . .

   . . . about God.

   . . . about myself.

   . . . about my motivations.

One thing I want to apply is:

Lord, I hope . . .

Lord, I need you to . . .

DAY 81_____

RIGHT THINKING

Thy word is a lamp to my feet, and a light to my path.
PSALM 119:105

MANY OF US ARE UNAWARE OF WHAT WE REALLY BELIEVE ABOUT God and about ourselves. We often say what we don't mean, and mean what we don't say. God's Word is our guide. And yet, we often experience difficulty in applying scriptural concepts to our lives because of the elaborate array of defenses we have structured over the years to protect ourselves. It is important to understand that Scripture can be used to identify and attack these defensive barriers, enabling us to experience an open and honest relationship with God:

For the word of God is living and active and sharper than any two-edged sword, and piercing as far as the division of soul and spirit, of both joints and marrow, and able to judge the thoughts and intentions of the heart. And there is no creature hidden from His sight, but all things are open and laid bare to the eyes of Him with whom we have to do.
HEBREWS 4:12–13

• Describe how your thoughts and beliefs have been developed. (Include the influences of society, your family background, experiences, relationships):

• Read 2 Timothy 3:16–17 and explain how the Scriptures can affect our thinking and our lives:

As I read in Your Word today, Father, please show me . . .

Day 82 _____

TIME

Not that I have already obtained all this, or have already been made perfect, but I press on to take hold of that for which Christ Jesus took hold of me. Brothers, I do not consider myself yet to have taken hold of it. But one thing I do: Forgetting what is behind and straining toward what is ahead, press on toward the goal to win the prize for which God has called me heavenward in Christ Jesus.

PHILIPPIANS 3:12–14

IF WE WERE COMPUTERS, SOLUTIONS TO OUR PROBLEMS WOULD be produced in microseconds. People, however, don't change that quickly. The agrarian metaphors given in the Scriptures depict *seasons* of planting, weeding, watering, growth, and harvesting. Farmers don't expect to plant seeds in the morning and harvest their crops that afternoon. Seeds must go through a complete cycle of growth, receiving plenty of attention in the process, before they mature. In this age of instant coffee, microwave dinners, and instant banking, we tend to assume that spiritual, emotional, and relational health will be instantaneous. These unrealistic expectations only cause discouragement and disappointment.

Some of us seem to respond to this environment of growth very quickly; others, after a few weeks or months; and still others, never at all. Why the difference? Why are some of us able to apply principles of growth so much more readily than others?

Some of us are in situations where one or more elements of growth are in some way missing or lacking. We may be trying to deal with our difficulties alone. We may be depending on a rigid structure of discipline for positive change, instead of blending a healthy combination of our responsibility with the Holy Spirit's enabling power. We may be expecting too much too soon, and may be experiencing disappointment with our slow results. Some of us may, in fact, be ready to quit the growth process entirely.

- Why do we often tend to expect fast results when we begin to seek growth and change in our lives?

- Why is it important for us to have Paul's process-perspective about life (Philippians 3:12–14)?

Father, I rest in the knowledge that if I stay sincerely focused upon You, I will move forward in my growth process at the pace of Your perfect timing . . .

Day 83 _____

THE LONG JOURNEY

Not that I have already obtained it, or have already become perfect, but I press on in order that I may lay hold of that for which also I was laid hold of by Christ Jesus.
PHILIPPIANS 3:12

OUR GROWTH TOWARD WHOLENESS AND MATURITY IS A JOURNEY which won't be completed until we join the Lord in heaven. The Apostle Paul understood this, and saw himself as being in the middle of this process.

If Paul, the foremost missionary and writer of much of the New Testament, saw himself as being "in the process," we can be encouraged to continue in the process toward change as well. It will help to have reasonable expectations about our progress. Sometimes, we will experience flashes of insight and spurts of growth, but the process of healing and renewal will more often be slow and methodical. Our emotions, too, may occasionally be very pleasant and positive, but when God's light shines on another area of hurt in our lives, we will likely experience another round of pain and anger. Remember that healing can only continue as we put ourselves in an environment characterized by honesty, affirming relationships, right thinking, the Holy Spirit's love and power, and time.

_____

- Describe how your emotions might change over the course of a year or two of healing:

Lord, I am thankful for the opportunities You have given me to renew myself, to learn a better way of living, and to relate well with others . . .

DAY 84 _____

NEW LIFE

For we also once were foolish ourselves, disobedient,
deceived, enslaved to various lusts and pleasures,
spending our life in malice and envy, hateful, hating one
another. But when the kindness of God our Savior and His
love for mankind appeared, He saved us, not on the basis
of deeds which we have done in righteousness, but
according to His mercy, by the washing of regeneration and
renewing by the Holy Spirit, whom He poured out upon us
richly through Jesus Christ our Savior, that being justified
by His grace we might be made heirs according to the hope
of eternal life.

TITUS 3:3–7

REGENERATION IS NOT A SELF-IMPROVEMENT PROGRAM, NOR IS
it a clean-up campaign for our sinful natures. *Regeneration*
is nothing less than the impartation of new life. As Paul
stated in Ephesians 2:5, we were once dead in our sins,
but have since been made alive in Christ.

Regeneration is the renewing work of the Holy Spirit
that literally makes each believer a new person at the
moment he or she trusts Christ as Savior.

In that wondrous, miraculous moment, we experience
more than swapping one set of standards for another. We
experience what Jesus called a new birth (John 3:3–6), a
Spirit-wrought renewal of the human spirit, a transform-

ing resuscitation which takes place so that the Spirit is alive within us (Romans 8:10).

• What are some characteristics of "new life"?

As I rejoice in my "new life" and Your love, Jesus, I feel . . .

DAY 85 _____

THE APPROVAL ADDICT

For we are not bold to class or compare ourselves with some of those who commend themselves; but when they measure themselves by themselves, and compare themselves with themselves, they are without understanding.

2 CORINTHIANS 10:12

WE SPEND MUCH OF OUR TIME BUILDING RELATIONSHIPS, striving to please people and win their respect. And yet, after all of our sincere, conscientious effort, it takes only one unappreciative word from someone to ruin our sense of self-worth. How quickly an insensitive word can destroy the self-assurance we've worked so hard to achieve!

The world we live in is filled with people who demand that we please them in exchange for their approval and acceptance. Such demands often lead us directly to a second false belief: *I must be approved by certain others to feel good about myself.*

We are snared by this lie in many subtle ways. Believing it causes us to bow to peer pressure in an effort to gain approval. We may join clubs and organizations, hoping to find a place of acceptance for ourselves. We often identify ourselves with social groups, believing that being with others like ourselves will assure our acceptance and their approval.

205

Many people have admitted that their experimentation with drugs or sex is a reaction to their need to belong. However, drugs and sexual promiscuity promise something they can't fulfill, and experimentation only leaves these people with pain, and usually, a deeper need for self-worth and acceptance.

———————

• How does the fear of rejection affect your behavior?

Father, sometimes people and situations can be so frustrating. I need to be more concerned about what You think of me—what I'm doing, saying, thinking, feeling—instead of allowing myself to be influenced by the opinions of others . . .

JOURNAL _____ WEEK 17

From my reflection this week, I learned . . .

    . . . about God.

    . . . about myself.

    . . . about my motivations.

One thing I want to apply is:

Lord, I hope . . .

Lord, I need you to . . .

DAY 86 _____

RECOILING FROM LOVE

And if one can overpower him who is alone, two can
resist him. A cord of three strands is not quickly torn apart.
ECCLESIASTES 4:12

INSTEAD OF BEING REFRESHED BY THE TRUTH OF GOD'S LOVE, IF
we have been deeply wounded, we may recoil from it,
believing that we are unlovable. We may be fearful of
reaching out and being hurt again. Whatever the cause,
the result is withdrawal from the very idea of being loved
and accepted.

Those who have received poor parental modeling
need new models—loving Christian friends—to experience
the love and grace of God. Through His body of believers,
God often provides us with models of His love, so that our
perception of His character can be slowly reshaped into
one that is more accurate, resulting in a healthier
relationship with Him. Then, our deep emotional, spiritual,
and relational wounds can begin to heal, and we can more
fully experience God's unconditional love.

Some of us are already involved in strong
relationships with people who are understanding and
patient with us; some of us haven't yet been able to
cultivate relationships like these, and are still looking. If
this is your situation, you may need to find a pastor or
counselor who can help you get started, possibly by

directing you to one or more believers who can minister to you. A small fellowship group or Bible study is often an excellent resource for intimate sharing, comfort, and encouragement. If you have tried to cultivate healthy relationships, but haven't found any yet, don't give up! The Lord wants all of us to be in an environment where we can experience more of His love through our relationships with other believers.

If you ask God for guidance, and are willing to continue putting forth the effort, He will lead you to some people who can provide this kind of an environment for you in His perfect time.

- What are some reasons people might be afraid of being loved and recoil from those who love them?

- Are any of these true of you? If so, which ones? How do these affect your self-esteem, your behavior, and your relationships?

Dear God, I am grateful to You for leading me to relationships that are healthy and fulfilling. I'm so comforted to know that You are aware of how vulnerable I am and will be standing beside me as I reach out to others . . .

DAY 87 _____

RESPONDING TO UNBELIEVERS

But I say to you who hear, love your enemies, do good
to those who hate you, bless those who curse you, pray for
those who mistreat you.

LUKE 6:27–28

BUT WHAT ABOUT OUR RESPONSE TO UNBELIEVERS? ALTHOUGH
they haven't yet trusted in the cross of Christ for the removal
of their condemnation before God, Jesus was very clear
about how we are to treat them. In Matthew 22:37, 39, He
told His disciples to *love the Lord your God, with all your
heart, and with all your soul, and with all your mind,* and to
love your neighbor (both believers and unbelievers) *as
yourself.* Christ didn't come to love and die for the lovely,
righteous people of the world. If He had, we would all be in
trouble! Instead, He came to love and die for the unrighteous,
the inconsiderate, and the selfish. As we grow in our understanding of His love for us, and continue to grasp that He has
rescued us from the righteous condemnation we deserve
because of our sins, we will gradually become more patient
and kind to others when they fail. It can be very helpful if we
compare the failure or sin of others with our sin that Christ
died to forgive: *There is nothing that anyone can do to me
that can compare with my sin of rebellion that Christ has
completely forgiven.* That should give us a lot of perspective!

_____

211

- Does the passage in Luke 6 mean you should deny the heat of others' offenses toward you and excuse them? Why, or why not?

- What is the proper blend of honesty, forgiveness, boundaries in relationships, and love?

Heavenly Father, I want to obey Your Word from Matthew 22:37, 39. I do love You with all my heart, soul, and mind. Sometimes I need an extra portion of Your help, though, when it comes to "love your neighbor as yourself." If I am to become more consistent in following this command, I need to . . .

DAY 88_____

STOP BLAMING!

And He is the radiance of His glory and the exact
representation of His nature, and upholds all things by the
word of His power. When He had made purification of sins,
He sat down at the right hand of the Majesty on high.
HEBREWS 1:3

SOME OF US HAVE A TENDENCY TO PERCEIVE OF JESUS AS OUR
friend, and God as a harsh disciplinarian. Yet the author
of Hebrews described Jesus as *the radiance of [God's] glory
and the exact representation of His nature* (Hebrews 1:3).

Studying passages like these and spending time with
compassionate, forgiving Christians has enabled the Holy
Spirit to reshape my perception of God over the years. I
continue to experience remorse when I fail. But rather
than hide from God, fearing His punishment, I more often
approach Him with appreciation for what His love has
accomplished for me.

Both assuming and assigning blame for failure can
have a number of detrimental consequences. Many
psychologists today adhere to a theory called Rational
Emotive Therapy. This very helpful theory states that
blame is the core of most emotional disturbances. The
answer, they insist, is for each of us to stop blaming
ourselves and others, and learn to accept ourselves in
spite of our imperfections. How right they are! Christ's

213

death is the complete payment for sin, and we can claim His complete forgiveness and acceptance daily.

A number of emotional problems are rooted in the false belief that we must meet certain standards to be acceptable, and that the only way to deal with inadequacies is to punish ourselves and others for them. There is no way we can shoulder such a heavy burden. Our guilt will overpower us, and the weight of our failures will break us.

The false belief, *Those who fail (including myself) are unworthy of love and deserve to be punished,* is at the root of our fear of punishment and our propensity to punish others.

———————

• How deeply are you affected by this lie?

• How does blaming others affect you? Your relationships?

Jesus, help me to accept others today as I would want them to accept me. I need to remember that I can make mistakes just as easily as they can . . .

DAY 89 _____

PROPITIATION

By this the love of God was manifested in us, that God has sent His only begotten Son into the world so that we might live through Him. In this is love, not that we loved God, but that He loved us and sent His Son to be the propitiation for our sins. Beloved, if God so loved us, we also ought to love one another.

1 JOHN 4:9–11

WHEN CHRIST DIED ON THE CROSS, HE WAS OUR SUBSTITUTE. He took upon Himself the righteous wrath of God that we deserved. The depth of God's love for us is revealed by the extremity of His actions for us: the holy Son of God became a man and died a horrible death in our place. A passage written by Isaiah, who anticipated the coming of Christ, states:

Surely our griefs He Himself bore,
    and our sorrows He carried;
yet we ourselves esteemed Him stricken,
    smitten of God, and afflicted.
But He was pierced through for our transgressions,
    He was crushed for our iniquities;
the chastening for our well-being fell upon Him,
    and by His scourging we are healed.

All of us like sheep have gone astray,
   each of us has turned to his own way;
but the Lord has caused the iniquity of us all to fall on
   Him.

ISAIAH 53:4–6

- Is it hard for you to realize that you deserved the wrath of God for your sin? Why or why not?

- How do you feel when you realize that His worth has been replaced by His love for you?

Thank You, Lord, for . . .

DAY 90_____

HIS GREAT LOVE

But God, being rich in mercy, because of His great love
with which He loved us, even when we were dead in our
transgressions, made us alive together with Christ (by
grace you have been saved), and raised us up with Him,
and seated us with Him in the heavenly places, in Christ
Jesus, in order that in the ages to come He might show the
surpassing riches of His grace in kindness toward us in
Christ Jesus. For by grace you have been saved through
faith; and that not of yourselves, it is the gift of God; not as
a result of works, that no one should boast.

EPHESIANS 2:4–9

BECAUSE WE ARE HIS CHILDREN, PERFORMANCE IS NO LONGER
the basis of our worth. We are unconditionally and deeply
loved by God, and we can live by faith in His grace. We
were spiritually dead, but the Lord has made us alive and
has given us the high status of sonship to the Almighty
God. It will take all of eternity to comprehend the wealth
of His love and grace.

Propitiation, then, means that Christ has satisfied
the holy wrath of God through His payment for sin. There
was only one reason for Him to do this: He loves us;
infinitely, eternally, unconditionally, irrevocably, He loves
us. God the Father loves us with the love of a father,
reaching to snatch us from harm. God the Son loves us

217

with the love of a brother, laying down His life for us. He alone has turned away God's wrath from us. There is nothing we can do, no amount of good deeds we can accomplish, and no religious ceremonies we can perform that can pay for our sins. Instead, Christ has conclusively paid for them so that we can escape eternal condemnation and experience His love and purposes both now and forever.

Christ not only paid for our sins at one point in time, but continues to love us and teach us day after day. We have a weapon to use against Satan as he attacks us with doubts about God's love for us. Our weapon is the fact that Christ took our punishment upon Himself at Calvary. We no longer have to fear punishment for our sins because Christ paid for them all—past, present, and future. This tremendous truth of propitiation clearly demonstrates that we are truly and deeply loved by God. His perfect love casts out all fear as we allow it to flood our hearts (1 John 4:18).

––––––––––

• What factors can contribute to you experiencing more and more of God's love and grace?

Dear Father, there is no greater love than Yours. I am forever grateful to You for my salvation, for my freedom from guilt and condemnation, for Your unconditional love and acceptance of me . . .

JOURNAL _____ WEEK 18

From my reflection this week, I learned . . .

    . . . about God.

    . . . about myself.

    . . . about my motivations.

One thing I want to apply is:

Lord, I hope . . .

Lord, I need you to . . .

Robert S. McGee is a professional counselor and lecturer who has helped thousands of people experience the love and acceptance of Jesus Christ. He is also the Founder and President of Rapha.

Rapha is the nation's largest manager of inpatient psychiatric care and substance abuse treatment from a distinctively Christian perspective. In hospitals located nationwide, Rapha offers a full range of care for adults and adolescents.

SUGGESTED READING _____

Many people have benefited from using Robert S. McGee's best seller, *The Search for Significance* in small groups. The truths presented in this book/workbook form the foundational cornerstones that provide the balance of spiritual and clinical therapy in the Rapha Treatment Center program.

Rapha Resources' books, workbooks, videos, and audio cassettes provide practical, biblically sound information and encouragement for people who struggle with family of origin issues, low self-esteem, codependency, sexual abuse, depression, eating disorders, chemical dependency, marriage and family issues, inordinate fear, and bitterness. These materials are designed to be used by individuals as well as in support groups. Excellent group leaders' guides and training materials are also available. Call 1 (800) 460-HOPE for a free catalog.